Tragedy, Survival, and Triumph

A Memoir

William Cowell Duckworth

Copyright © 2024 by William Cowell Duckworth

Published by Sandi Huddleston-Edwards, Publisher
Here I Am Publishing, LLC.
780 Monterrosa Drive
Myrtle Beach, SC 29572
704-604-7265

All rights reserved. No part of this book may be reproduced or transmitted in any form or by any electronic or mechanical means, including photocopying, recording, or by any information storage and retrieval system, without the written permission of the publisher, except where permitted by law.

ISBN: 978-1-958032-05-3

Edited by Yvette Kilgore, Editor, Here I Am Publishing, LLC
Edited by Jane Lentz, Editor, Here I Am Publishing, LLC
Cover design by Jeremy Cannada
Page composition by Levi Stephen at 303 Pixels LLC (303pixels.com)

Keith Jacobs, Photographer
Coharie Ventures, Inc.
Keithjacobs@coharieventures.com

This book is a work of non-fiction. Some names, characters, places, and incidents have been changed to protect identities. Permissions have been obtained from those in the story and borrowed information has been cited and noted accordingly.

A product of the United States of America.

Dedication

This book is dedicated to Carrie Campen

Acknowledgements

I would like to acknowledge my sister Mary Lynn, and my "anonymous source" for providing valuable information that helped tell my story more accurately.

Contents

Foreword ix

Prologue xi

Chapter 1
    Backstory — Leading up to When I Was Born 1

Chapter 2
    Thrust Into the Dawn of a New Life 13

Chapter 3
    Destination Denver, Difficult Times, and Bullies 19

Chapter 4
    The Disparaging Father 25

Chapter 5
    Starting School and Coping with Additional Bullies 35

Chapter 6
    The Worst Day of My Life 41

Chapter 7
    Homelife and the Makings of an Unhappy Childhood. 45

Chapter 8
    OCD Prison, A Life Sentence 49

Chapter 9
    Sides of My Mother
    (Dual Personalities, Time Controller and Insensitivity) 65

Chapter 10
    The High School Years/Unlucky in Love 79

Chapter 11
    Stonehenge 93

Contents

Chapter 12
    The College Years..103

Chapter 13
    Thrown to the Wolves 121

Chapter 14
    Danger Zone—Playing with Fire 131

Chapter 15
    Detour..151

Chapter 16
    The Premonition 159

Chapter 17
    Dealing with Another Tragedy/Coping with
    Awkward Family Matters......................................163

Chapter 18
    Cause of the Crash of EgyptAir Flight 990 and Greed.........169

Chapter 19
    Trying to Move Forward By Climbing Emotional Mountains ...181

Chapter 20
    Poetic Justice 187

Chapter 21
    Shaken to the Core 195

Chapter 22
    Jack Pot City..201

Chapter 23
    The Dawning of a New and Happy Life................207

Epilogue: After-Thoughts and Reflections......................211
Resources 215
About the Author 219

Foreword

I was honored when William C. Duckworth asked me to write the foreword for his autobiography. It is my privilege to do so.

I have known the author, William C. Duckworth (Bill), for close to fifty years. Fast friends we were not, but best friends we became. While our friendship has waned over the past years for a number of reasons (COVID, health issues with both of us, etc.), we still maintain regular contact, even with the distance between us (Myrtle Beach, SC-Denver, CO). Far from being self-righteous and far from being perfect individuals, the one common bond weaved throughout our years of friendship is honesty, a trait that gives authenticity to the book, perhaps to even a shocking degree to readers.

When Bill told me he was writing an autobiography, I was highly skeptical. My immediate thoughts and questions were how and why. The how was answered in Bill's meeting a book writer, publisher, editor, and teacher, Sandi Huddleston-Edwards. The why? For various and numerous personal reasons. Bill has always thought he had a story to tell because of how unique his life story is. At the behest and encouragement of his long-time therapist, Carrie, Bill's own motivation to share his life story, and the coincidental meeting of Sandi Huddleston-Edwards, Bill's autobiography was born.

Bill's goal in writing his autobiography is to help inspire readers of any background to overcome life's most challenging obstacles.

In Bill's case, it was multiple horrific family tragedies, parental and family dysfunction, bullying, relationships issues, crippling depression, and obsessive-compulsive disorder (OCD).

Bill's storytelling of his life is frank, transparent, and courageously honest, and at times, very raw and sometimes graphic. He is able, somehow, to find humor in some of the obstacles he faced. This gives the readers another peek into his personality. There are no filters in his autobiography. None.

While hoping to help and inspire readers to overcome their own problems and obstacles, he also educates and informs them about what has been a large and difficult part of his life: OCD.

Among many other issues, I remember vividly in the early years of our friendship, Bill's incessant hand washing, his constant checking of doors and windows to ensure they were locked, and his constant need to be reassured by me that he had not hit anything in going through intersections. When my reassurances were not convincing enough, Bill would turn the car around and retrace the streets we just traveled on to ensure he had, in fact, not hit anybody and/or anything.

All of this had me quietly thinking, *what is wrong with this guy?* Eventually, as our friendship grew stronger and Bill became more knowledgeable about OCD, he became comfortable with discussing his condition. Through Bill's honesty, frankness, and openness, no matter how difficult the topic of OCD was for him to discuss, I began to learn about the condition. Many, many years have passed since I first heard about OCD from Bill. I have learned much more about the subject over that time through Bill and news/magazine articles. Do I know everything there is to know about OCD? No, I don't, not even close.

I do, however, have a keen awareness and appreciation for the life Bill has lived while fighting OCD every inch of the way. So, too, will you after reading Bill's life story.

Living with and managing OCD is incredibly only part of Bill's unique life journey. Yet it is with that same determination and perseverance that Bill faced down other life's tragedies: his difficult days, weeks, and years of unyielding depression, and the disappointments, difficulties, and regrets in his life that he has so openly and magically shared with you, the reader. His pride in overcoming and ultimately prevailing over everything that he has faced in life brilliantly shines through in this autobiography, and rightfully so.

Indeed, a life of *Tragedy, Survival and Triumph* is Bill Duckworth's life. Here now is Bill's story.

— TIMOTHY M. CALLANAN

Prologue

It was January 11, 1960, seven miles north of Athens, Georgia, on U.S. Highway 29, when my life would change in a negative way forever. We were traveling across the country. My father, Robert Elmer Cowell (age 36); my mother, Eloise Kilby Cowell (age 33); and my sister, Mary Lynn Cowell (age 4). I was the fourth member of the family, only nine months old. They had named me William Edward Cowell.

We had just left the hotel, traveling in my father's Mercedes-Benz 180D. We were headed to Washington, DC, where my father, a Lieutenant Commander in the Navy, was under orders to report for a new post at the Pentagon, where he was assigned.

On that dreadful Monday morning, my life would change course from what it was expected to be. That day, a new trajectory sent my life into uncharted territory.

It was approximately 7:15 a.m. when all HELL broke loose as we suddenly approached a curve in the road. A vehicle coming from the opposite direction, driven by Barry E. Brown, 27, of Athens, GA, was on bald, thin tires, traveling at a high rate of speed. He lost control going into the curve, "swung wide," and swerved, crossing the center of the road, then *WHAM*! He struck our car head-on. The inertia sent our car in reverse thirty-six feet. The metal-to-metal hit was an extremely hard impact. My father was dead, my mother was dead, and Barry Brown was dead. I'm told, both my parents were thrust through the windshield and upon impact, both my parents were reported to have been "instantly killed." The only survivors were my sister and me. We were suddenly orphaned. I was found on the front passenger floor. Unfortunately, there were no seat belts in our car ("3 Die in Auto Wreck;" "Lcdr., Mrs. Cowell killed in accident").

Barry Brown ruined many more lives that fateful day than just the people he killed. He had caused a chain of events that would turn dreadfully horrible for many, many years to come for my sister and me.

After the accident happened near someone's front yard, my sister gave the state patrol, who had arrived upon the deadly gruesome accident scene, information about our relatives to contact. According to the *Pittsburgh Post-Gazette*, my sister and I were taken to Athens General Hospital "...in serious condition with possible skull fractures" ("S.E. Cowell's Navy Son and Wife Die in Crash"). I also suffered a broken arm.

Our parents' funeral was held at the "...Fort Myer Chapel and burial at Arlington National Cemetery" in Washington, DC ("Arlington Burial Set for Cowell and Wife"). They were buried together in the same grave, one casket stacked on top of the other. This is done when a spouse of military personnel dies to save space in the cemetery for future decedents.

Now a dilemma arose. Who would raise my sister and me? My father and his sister, my aunt Allison, had made an earlier agreement that if for any reason one of them died young, the other sibling would raise the other one's children. Unfortunately, that reality did not come to fruition the way it had been planned. The timing was off because Allison was in the hospital, having just had serious surgery, unable to attend the funeral, and was not in proper physical condition to take on two additional children. She and her husband already had two of their own they were trying to raise.

Therefore, initially, my paternal grandfather S.E. Cowell was awarded my sister and me. Options now had to be evaluated. My maternal grandfather Herbert Duckworth was of the belief that the court should decide our fate.

My father was a graduate of Annapolis Naval Academy in Annapolis, Maryland. One of my father's classmates was Stansfield Turner, who was appointed CIA Director under President Jimmy Carter. Mr. Turner had heard about the accident and wrote a letter and offered to raise the two of us.

Infighting began to occur between the Cowells and the Duckworths, and it got nasty. My paternal grandfather, S.E. Cowell, really wanted us

Prologue

to go to my aunt Allison and her family. Allison also really wanted us even though it would create an extra burden on her family to raise four children.

My grandfather Cowell thought long and hard and reluctantly decided to bestow the task of raising us to my mother's younger brother, John Duckworth, and his wife, Jan Duckworth, both of whom were thirty-one years old, because they were unable to have children themselves.

That decision would turn out to be extremely unfortunate in my sister's eyes and mine. This is a story I feel needs to be told. You will discover the reasons for my title: *Tragedy, Survival, and Triumph*.

Photo was taken in the late 1990s. The first and only time our immediate family members gathered together since the fatal car accident on January 11, 1960.

"My soul was born at the beach!"

— WILLIAM COWELL DUCKWORTH

Chapter 1

Backstory — Leading up to When I Was Born

The journey you are about to embark on is a detailed accounting of my life. I have suffered from the untimely deaths of immediate family members, a mental condition (for which there is no cure), mass rejection by women, extreme depression, devastating heartache over a lost love, and a quest searching to find myself over the course of a lifetime.

To be quite honest, I do not have much information about my biological parents as information about them was rarely shared with me. I found that quite unsettling throughout my life. The only information I have is from some old family papers, newspaper articles, photographs, and limited vague short stories relatives have told me.

In my adoptive family, there was an understanding that we were not really at liberty to discuss the topic of my biological parents. If we ever did and asked any questions, my adoptive parents would respond with short and to-the-point concise answers and would *never* elaborate. This I have always *RESENTED!* If I were in my adoptive parents' shoes, I would have been more than happy to answer any and all questions in detail. I have a *right* to know as much as possible about each of my biological parents. That *right* was denied to me.

My adoptive parents John and Jan Duckworth (John being the younger brother of my biological mother) were not able to have children. I learned this in high school when I asked my adopted mom why they did not have children of their own. I think in their minds, they wanted to feel that my sister and I were their legitimate children and tried to raise us as such. I have so longed to know all the details of my biological parents, what their personalities were like, their likes and dislikes, and if I shared anything in common with them, such as personality traits. As you read on, this is the *little* I know about each of them.

My biological mother, Eloise Kilby Duckworth, was born on December 1, 1927. Kilby is a family surname from one of my relatives on my maternal grandfather's side. My mother went by the name Kilby. She was the daughter of a career NAVAL father, Herbert Spencer Duckworth, who was a fighter pilot in the Navy and worked his way up to Vice Admiral before retiring. I've always known him as *Grandpa Ducky*.

These men were in the movie Hell Divers, which featured Clark Gable, third from the left. My grandfather actually flew the plane that Gable was supposed to be flying. Grandfather Duckworth is second from the right.

In World War II, Grandpa Ducky took part in the battle of the Coral Sea in the Pacific. He worked on the film *HELL DIVERS* with Clark Gable. My grandfather was the man who made Clark Gable look good when he was flying the plane. You see, my grandfather was actually flying the plane for Gable. Note the photo of my grandfather with a mustache less Clark Gable, together with some others on the film set. This film came out eight years prior to *Gone with the Wind*.

Years later, Grandpa Ducky was given command of the USS Midway, where he was given the assignment "Operation Frostbite." Commencing on March 1, 1946, his mission was to take the new carrier on a "...test voyage into sub-arctic conditions in Canadian waters to evaluate the feasibility of conducting carrier operations in extreme cold." The ship was taken as far north "in the icy waters of the Davis Straits between Labrador and Greenland." During the mission, they encountered adverse conditions, such as "...high winds, heavy seas, snow, and green water over the bow." They even came across icebergs. They tested helicopters and jet flights for the first time in these adverse conditions and other operations (Zingheim).

"Although World War II had just ended six months earlier, Navy planners were..." concerned about possible warfare with the Soviet Union (Zingheim). Cruising at such high latitudes, Soviet targets would be within reach with an aircraft carrier. It was hoped that operating in winter conditions would work to the advantage of the Navy.

Later, my grandfather relinquished command to his successor. Today the USS Midway is retired and currently rests in San Diego Bay and is open for tourism. His photo can be found on the upper decks alongside all the others who commanded the ship before it was retired. I have visited that ship twice. At one time, my grandfather held a position at the Pentagon in Washington, DC. I never got to know him well, as he and my adopted dad never got along very well, much like the relationship I had with my adoptive dad. So, I knew my grandfather slightly better than an acquaintance but never much beyond that.

From what I have been able to piece together about my mother through researching newspaper articles, hearing family stories, and looking through her senior year class yearbook of 1946, I was able to learn more about who she was as a person.

She attended Coronado High School in Coronado, California. She seemed to be quite popular with the boys, based on all the signed well wishes and was one of the senior class officers. She was involved in many of the school's clubs and activities. She was the type of girl I disliked when I was in high school, as I was not popular, was bullied, and had few friends. These girls were the snobby ones who hung out with the popular boys like the football players and such. These girls would never notice someone so far down on the totem pole as I was.

Around the age of forty-two, I found out through a relative that my mother had once been a model for a large modeling agency. *WHAT?* Why was I never told this before? It was just more resentment that bothered me, not knowing these interesting details about my own mother. Outside of that, I don't know much else about my mother, I'm sad to say.

My father, Robert Elmer Cowell, was born June 12, 1924, in Pennsylvania. He seemed to get along with his parents very well; he and my Aunt Allison, his sibling, grew up in a wonderful family atmosphere, with my father highly respecting his father and having a great relationship with him. A far cry from what I was dealt with by the adoption of my new father, John Duckworth, who was technically my blood uncle.

My biological father grew up taking a very active role in serious swimming. I don't know how it came about, but once visiting my sister in Morocco, where she now lives, we were going through some old family letters and things my father had written to his parents. The letters revealed that my father was up early in the mornings in high school to practice swimming at the pool. Then, after school, he was back at the pool practicing more of his swimming. He apparently became quite good at it. He went on to college, setting records against other Ivy League schools, winning trophies, and going on to win the silver medal in swimming the backstroke in the 1948 Olympics in London.

My father's first year of college was spent at Penn State, and he joined the Alpha Tau Omega fraternity, the same fraternity his father had joined when he was in college. I came across a paper my father had written about his first year of college at Penn State. It looked like it was written for an English class assignment. It was dated October 6, 1943. In that paper, he states how much he desires to attend the Naval Academy in Annapolis, Maryland.

As Christmas vacation approached, he knew he was having trouble maintaining good-quality grades due to the swim meets and fraternity activities. He knew that in order to get into the Naval Academy, he would have to have high marks. He seemed to have a particularly hard time with chemistry. He even weighed the option that was the toughest decision of his college year. Should he just throw in the towel and say screw it, as others were doing, or should he buckle down and learn that chemistry? He did the difficult thing and dug in and *learned* that chemistry.

As a result, he swam seldom, played less, and studied, studied, and studied that chemistry, and when it came to taking the test, he was rewarded with a good grade. Christmas vacation came, and he returned home.

The following semester, swimming was at hand again, and his grades weren't what he had hoped. His swimming coach, who was also an English teacher, had a profound influence on him that it seemed he never forgot.

My father was practicing swimming with such great vigor that he found himself too tired to study in the evenings, and then more swimming meets came along. Luck was with my father as he wrote in his college paper, "Four races and four new records. Three times I had lowered the Eastern Collegiate record" (Cowell). After swimming, "our invasion," as my father put it against Syracuse and Cornell, he and six of his swimming mates found themselves in the hospital in a siege of influenza. Once released, he mentions he did a very foolish thing. Within less than two hours, he found himself in another swim meet "against the boys from Temple," and two more races that same afternoon. The following week he came down with a fever and chills. "Marks fell still lower. If I didn't get into the Academy, I would have no civilian occupational interest, but Annapolis looked farther away than ever," he wrote (Cowell). Apparently, getting into the Naval Academy meant everything to my father to be a career Naval man.

Rutgers's swimming team then came to Penn State with what my father described as "its array of champions. The constant theme of friends' conversations was, 'Think you can beat last year's champion?' You see, I just had to swim" (Cowell). Still suffering from a "rasping chest" and coughing, my father felt "dejected" when he saw the team leave for the Eastern Collegiates. "A day later (at the constant urging of the athletic directors), I made the trip" he wrote (Cowell).

"Another victory and coughing [continued]" he wrote in his paper. From there, my father went on to the Nationals at Ohio State and won another medal. By this time, my father writes that his appointment to the Academy was coming through, and he was "over joyous" but still feared his grades were lacking and that he must do better (Cowell).

My father was finally appointed to the Naval Academy in Annapolis, Maryland, by the Honorable Thomas E. Scanlon of the 16th Congressional District of Pennsylvania. A newspaper article read as follows

Bob the son of S.E. Cowell, Sales Manager at the Eberhardt & Ober Brewing, is a graduate of Perry High School. He is the Allegheny Mountain Association Back-stroke swimming champion, the National Junior Champion, and holder of the Eastern Intercollegiate back-stoke record. He will enter Annapolis in June.... ("Appointed to Annapolis")

While at Annapolis, my father, on his 24th birthday (June 12), beat "the world 100- yard long-course backstroke swimming record today." "His time in the Naval Academy pool was 1 minute four-tenths second, against the old mark of 1 minute 2 seconds set by Al Vande Weghe, former Princeton swimmer, eight years ago" ("Cowell Breaks World Swim Record").

According to a newspaper article, "Annapolis Captain in Two Races," written by Jimmy Miller, my father at one time was "… the country's leading back-stroke swimmer." Miller goes on to say, "Bob, who has set all sorts of records in his two seasons at Annapolis is home…." He goes on to write, later in the article, "He is a national celebrity in the swimming world…. He is only 20 years old and is six feet three inches tall." My father also went on to become the Captain of the Naval Academy swim team (Miller).

My father graduated from the Naval Academy in 1946. Around 1947, T. J. Hamilton, Captain, U. S. Navy and Director of Football, had written a letter to my father that he was to be considered to compete in the 1948 Olympic Games in London, England. Hamilton was directed by the Superintendent of U. S. Naval Academy to nominate Navy personnel "who have an excellent chance of making the 1948 American Olympic team in several different sports" (Hamilton). My father was nominated, and the nomination was sent to the Secretary of the Navy. My father was selected to be on the U.S. Olympic swimming team for the 1948 games.

Once again, my father came through and won a silver medal for second place in the men's 100-meter backstroke, just short of winning first place by one-tenth of a second. Allen Stack was the man who beat my father with a time of 1:06.4. My father's time was 1:06.5. The race was so close that the judges were deadlocked in determining the winner. A "verdict had to be reached by computing the averages of the times shown by 10 stopwatches"

(Cope). According to the same article, my father did not contest the decision. "I swam my best race. I agree with the decision. I think Stack won" (Cope). Following the silver medal win, my father was approached to play Tarzan, according to what my aunt Allison told my sister. He turned that offer down to pursue his dream of a career in the Navy.

Once he graduated from the academy, my father was assigned to the USS Harry S. Truman. That's when he faced his first brush with death in February of 1952. It must have been a harrowing experience for him. At approximately 8:05 a.m., his Banshee jet "was catapulted too weakly from an air crafter carrier and plunged some 50 yards forward into the Caribbean Sea where it flipped over and sank" (Cope).

My father's plane only reached ninety knots. He realized he was going to have to ditch the plane. He concentrated on flying the plane as opposed to letting it stall. He set up a rate of descent and released the tip tanks. As he hit the sea, the "water came over the nose and the plane flipped on its back" (Cowell). He then released his shoulder harness and pushed free of the cockpit. However, in trying to escape, he felt something caught around his hips. He was able to free himself and suspected it might be his oxygen mask. Upon reaching the water's surface, he realized he was only fifty yards and slightly to the starboard side of the bow. The ship was moving toward him.

He swam the backstroke as rapidly as he could. At the same time, his parachute was a buoyant forceful drag. He was able to detach the parachute and inflate a floatation device. My father was twenty yards clear of the ship when the stern passed him by. A helicopter rescued him, and he safely returned to the ship.

My father had been offered another opportunity by the Navy to compete in the 1952 Olympic Games but declined. Now married, he could well see action in Korea soon. My father was quoted as saying (by the *Pittsburg Post-Gazette*), "Yes, I'd like to make the Olympic trip, but it seems to me there are more important things ahead than swimming" (Cope).

In the Navy in 1950, My father "became a naval pilot and was assigned to Red Ripper Fighter Squadron as public information and intelligence officer" (The Pittsburg Post-Gazette). The Red Rippers are a famous active fighter squadron. "He received two air medals and a letter of commendation

Pittsburgh District Olympic Album

Jet Pilot Bob Cowell Rejects Olympic Trip, Goes Off to War

There Are More Important Things, Says Swimmer

Last in a series of sketches of district Olympic competitors.

By MYRON COPE
Post-Gazette Sports Writer

Watching the sound, handsome body of a champion in action, it is thrilling to observe the graceful perfection with which it eludes the tackler, rolls with the foe's punch, kicks into full stride down the straightaway, or glides through the water. There is only one possible subtraction from the thrill, and that occurs if your mind reacts like the man who stands before a portrait of a beautiful woman and asks himself:

Would the spell be shattered if she opened her mouth?

It is a pathetic letdown to see a Jim Thorpe living clumsily as a professional parasite off public benevolence. But it is a satisfying experience to speak with another Olympian, young Bob Cowell, who has turned down a chance to swim in the Olympic Games again this summer because he thinks his country might be able to use him more advantageously in a war.

Declines Olympic Bid

Lieutenant Cowell is a tall, good-looking, 28-year-old Navy jet pilot who grew up in the Perrysville Avenue section of the Northside, later was graduated from the United States Naval Academy in 1946, then broke the world 100-yard backstroke record and missed winning the 1948 Olympic 100-meter title by one-tenth of a second. Cowell's Olympic race with Allen Stack, another United States Navy swimmer, was so close that the judges were deadlocked and the verdict had to be reached by computing the averages of the times shown by 10 stop watches. Stack's official time was declared to be 1:06.4, Cowell's 1:06.5.

Bob has no gripe.

"I swam my best race. I agree with the decision. I think Stack won."

The Navy recently invited Cowell to train for the '52 Olympics, but he declined. The famous Red Rippers fighters squadron, of which Bob, a married

UNSCHEDULED BATH — An alert Navy cameraman snapped this picture of Lieutenant Bob Cowell backstroking to safety after his plane failed in a take-off from a carrier and plunged into the Caribbean. Later, Cowell saw an enlargement of the photo and commented: "I'm looking at my feet as a good backstroker should."

Pittsburghers In Past Olympics

Following are the Pittsburgh district's competitors in past Olympic games.

TRACK AND FIELD
John Woodruff, Frank Jarvis, Hugh Lambie, Earl Johnson, Frank Shea, Joe Organ, Herb Douglas, Jack Weber, John Deni, Don Gwinn, Charles (Crip) Moore, and Vic Pickard.

BOXING
Jack Zivic, Pete Zivic, E. Greathouse and Carl (Rags) Madera.

SWIMMING
Lenore Kight Wingard, Susan Laird, Anna May Gorman, Bob Cowell, Adam Smith, Harry Clancy, and Paul Wyatt.

HOCKEY
Herbert Drury.

GYMNASTICS
George Wheeler

BOB COWELL
Duty first, then fun.

> **Texas League**
> YESTERDAY'S RESULTS
> 2—San Antonio .... Shreveport— 0
> 2—Fort Worth .... Oklahoma City— 1
> 5—Beaumont .... Houston— 1
> 5—Shreveport .... San Antonio— 3
> 11 innings.
>
> George Wheeler.
> SOCCER
> Archie Stremel, Stephen Grivnough, John (Zip) Zywan, Burkey Jones.
>
> ## YMHA Swimmers Romp To Victory at Clairton
>
> Ross McCarty, Al Wiggins, Diane Shepard Each Score Two Wins; Uniontown Second
>
> Swimmers from the YMHA dominated the swimming meet held at Clairton yesterday, scoring 72 points in the 13 events, 27 more than competitors from four other teams.
>
> Uniontown finished second with 17 points, Clairton scored 14, Allegheny Y nine, and Greensburg five.
>
> The YMHA scored slams in three events, and firsts in nine in splashing to an easy team victory. Only in the junior diving event did they fail to tally a point.
>
> Ross McCarty scored a double for YMHA men, winning the 86-yard and 215-yard free-style events. Al Wiggins won both the 129-yard men's individual medley and the 86-yard backstroke for men, and Diane Sheparo won the 80-yard and 43-yard free-style events for girls, both of YMHA.
>
> The Clairton pool is only 43 yards in length, accounting for the odd racing distances. Summary:
>
> 43-yard women's novice free-style—Won by Esther Fraher, Greensburg Y; second, Pat Cunningham, YMHA; third, Grace Zieles, YMHA. Time—32 seconds.
> 86-yard men's novice free-style—Won by Frank Lazarchak, YMHA; second, David Nida, Allegheny Y; third, Norman Bicer, YMHA. Time—56 seconds.
> 43-yard boys' free-style—Won by Ronald Dorsey, YMHA; second, Neal Connelly, Uniontown; third, James Fraley, Uniontown. Time—28 seconds.
> 43-yard girls' free-style—Won by Diane Shepard, YMHA; second, Mary Mulligan, YMHA; third, Audrey Shanaberger, Uniontown. Time—27.8 seconds.
> 86-yard men's backstroke—Won by Al Wiggins, YMHA; second, Tony Tresser, YMHA; third, Don Weber, YMHA. Time—56.4 seconds.
> 86-yard women's backstroke—Won by Audrey Shanaberger, Uniontown; second, Mary Sproul, Uniontown; third, Marcia Bradley, YMHA. Time—1:07.
> 86-yard men's free-style—Won by Ross McCarty, YMHA; second, John Rodgers, Clairton; third, Al Wiggins, YMHA. Time—47.4.
> 86-yard women's free-style—Won by Diane Shepard, YMHA; second, Mary Mulligan, YMHA; third, Betty Doying, YMHA. Time—1:01.5.
> 215-yard men's free-style—Won by Ross McCarty, YMHA; second, Tony Tresser, YMHA; third, John Martin, YMHA. No time.
> 129-yard men's individual medley—Won by Al Wiggins, YMHA; second, John Rodgers, Clairton; third, Ed Robsin, YMHA. No time.
> 86-yard women's breast stroke—Won by Shila Ostrow, YMHA; second, Beverly Sabol, Uniontown; third, Marcia Bradley, YMHA. No time.
> One-meter junior diving—Won by Milo Fischer, Allegheny Y, 204.55; second, Fred Ross, Clairton, 181.5; third, Ronald O'Brien, Allegheny Y, 178.40.
>
> man, is a member, could well be in Korean action soon.
> Without pomp he simply says, "Yes, I'd like to make the Olympic trip but it seems to me there are more important things ahead than swimming."
>
> **How He Escaped Death**
> Bob's swimming ability, it should be noted, was instrumental in his escape from a watery death in February of 1952 when his Banshee jet was catapulted, but too weakly, from an aircraft carrier and plunged some 50 yards forward into the Caribbean Sea where it flipped over and sank.
> Managing to struggle from the cockpit, Bob rose to the surface only to see the bow of the carrier bearing down on him, churning the water into a turbulence that could well have sucked in a lesser swimmer. But Bob, a form swimmer to the end, backstroked out of the danger zone as fast as he knew how. A helicopter dropped him a rope ladder by which he climbed to safety.
> It might be mentioned in conclusion that Lieutenant Cowell has accomplished the ultimate in naval tactics. His wife, the former Kilby Duckworth, is the daughter of an admiral—Admiral H. S. Duckworth, attached to the Pentagon.
>
> Biggie Munn, Michigan State football coach, has had the pleasure of watching five of his assistants move to head college coaching positions.

for service in the Mediterranean area and the Korean conflict" ("Services Arranged for Navy Couple Killed in Crash"). After the war, he became an instrument instructor in Japan and California. It sounds a bit like what Lieutenant Pete *Maverick* Mitchell chose to do in the first *Top Gun* film.

My father also appeared in *Look* magazine in the September 9, 1952, issue with Marilyn Monroe on the cover. The photo shows him getting into a fighter jet for an article on how the Navy and Air Force needed more pilots.

―◇―

The way my parents met was an interesting one. I don't know the full details, but my aunt Allison explained to me that my father was aware of my mother while possibly stationed at the same naval base. My

mother was not in the Navy but was obviously there because of Grandpa Ducky. My father had a keen eye for my mother and was trying to figure out how to meet her. Somehow my grandfather, H.S. Duckworth, caught wind of this. My grandfather must have obviously approved of my father. He arranged for my father to accompany his daughter, Eloise Kilby Duckworth, to an upcoming naval social event. Well, my father started to really worry because when a senior officer tells someone lower in command to accompany his daughter to one of these social events, that meant the daughter must be ugly and can't get a date.

My father was extremely pleased to find out it was actually my *MOTHER!* They married on January 12, 1950, at Maxwell Field, Montgomery, Alabama. One day shy of their tenth anniversary, they would be killed on January 11, 1960.

Years later, my sister was born in 1955, and I was born in 1959. Every year in my father's memory, the Naval Academy presents the Robert E. Cowell Award to the graduating midshipman, who has shown outstanding swimming ability, leadership, and good sportsmanship.

My biological parents on their Wedding Day.

My sister and me standing on the front porch of our home in Denver, circa 1965.

My biological mother and her brother, John, who became my adopted dad.

Chapter 2

Thrust Into the Dawn of a New Life

My grandfather Cowell had set up an estate account with a bank in Pennsylvania to handle the assets of my biological parents. The assets were divided equally between my sister and me. We would have access to the estate when we became of legal age. The ultimate decision came down to my grandpa Cowell, who would determine our upbringing. This is where it began to get ugly, and a fight between the Cowells and the Duckworths ensued, a milder version than the Hatfield's and McCoy's feud.

Grandfather Cowell started to play hardball. His preference was for us to be raised by my Aunt Allison's family. Aunt Allison really, really wanted us. However, her present health condition would create hardship for her family because Allison already had two children and would have to hire help if she took us on. Furthermore, it would create chaos in the current family dynamic.

John and Jan Duckworth wanted us, too. Grandpa Cowell weighed the options and, after deep thought, decided that since John and Jan couldn't have children, he would let them raise us. However, there were conditions placed on them at the time that were agreed to. One condition was that they would not be allowed to change our name from Cowell to Duckworth. Grandpa Cowell was very partial to the name Cowell.

This is where my story really begins.

Both my sister and I were sent to live with John and Jan Duckworth outside of Minneapolis, Minnesota, near White Bear Lake, in a residential community called North Oaks, which was also home to Walter Mondale.

John Duckworth worked for Armco Steel, Sheffield Division, as a District Manager in the Minneapolis/St. Paul area office. His wife, Jan, worked at a children's nursery. They had met in Kansas City at a party. John, at the time, was working for Armco Steel's home office in Kansas City, MO. Jan (maiden name Fairlamb) at the time was also working in Kansas City for TWA as a lead instructor of stewardess training, having been a previous stewardess with the airline in years prior. They were married three months later in Jan's hometown of Delta, Colorado, on September 2, 1956.

They had a beautiful new house built in the North Oaks neighborhood on a couple of acres that backed up to a small lake that was shared with other homes. I became very fond of that home and still miss it today.

The house was built into a side of a hill so that the front appeared to be ranch-style, and the back had a walk-out basement facing a downhill slope with a nice green lawn leading to the lake. There were many wonderful natural trees around parts of the property. I remember the interior floor plan so vividly. We had a living room picture window overlooking the big backyard down to the lake. We would use that backyard slope in the winter to sled down and ice skate on the frozen lake. I was too young to remember how cold the winters must have been, but I mainly have many fond memories in the summertime there. I so loved living at that house; I remember being happy there.

Meanwhile, John and Jan wanted a real family and were caught in limbo. If John and Jan remained as just guardians, problems could arise. For example, what if we needed medical treatment like an operation? They could not legally give consent. Not only that, but it would create a problem for me, as well as my sister. We would have to go through life explaining that we don't have any parents, just guardians. This would be tough to deal with going through K-12, which would cause us many times over the years having to explain our situation to other kids and the public, as well when it was none of their business.

Grandfather Fairlamb, Jan's father, was a lawyer in Delta, Colorado. He explained to John and Jan that my sister and I were living in an unsatisfactory arrangement that could be only temporary. One reason is because we could be taken away from them. Therefore, he strongly suggested that John and Jan proceed to adopt us.

John and Jan went forth and started the adoption proceedings. John had informed Grandfather Cowell, which did not sit well with him. Not at all. Grandpa Cowell accused my future adopted parents of breaking the agreement John and Jan previously agreed to and asked them to reconsider. My grandfather Cowell wrote a letter I found in the old family papers. He accused John and Jan of breaking the agreement to keep the Cowell name. Keeping the Cowell surname did not make good sense. Again, from the standpoint in the future, we'd have explaining to do. I can only assume Grandfather Cowell did not want our surnames changed because he wanted me to carry on the family name. Lawyers on both the Duckworth and the Cowell side got involved. Grandfather Cowell even went so far as to make a threat. I remember in the 1990s, I came across a letter from him circa 1960 or 1961 where he stated that if our names were changed to Duckworth, he would no longer have anything to do with us. He also would cut both of us out of his last will and testament. Grandfather Cowell used us as pawns—bargaining chips. When I came across this letter, it angered me. Grandfather Fairlamb knew there was real bad blood developing between the two families. Grandfather Fairlamb urged John and Jan to move forward with the adoption despite the threats from Grandfather Cowell because there needed to be love in our newfound family, and it would be the only assured way John and Jan could permanently keep us without the threat or worry that we'd be taken from them. This would undoubtedly make my life and my sister's life easier being adopted by completely eliminating any confusion and embarrassment by not having to explain to people why we didn't have any parents. I think John and Jan did the right thing by adopting us.

After a bitter fight that lasted twenty-one months, on September 27, 1961, my sister and I were officially adopted, and my name was changed from William Edward Cowell to William Cowell Duckworth. Cowell was used as my middle name in memory of my deceased parents. I like that surname for my middle name; it sounds classy, in my opinion. It's similar to Ronald Wilson Reagan.

Grandfather Cowell stayed true to his word and had nothing to do with me for the rest of his life. However, every Christmas year, he would send me a fifty-dollar check. But that was it. Nothing more. Why would my grandfather Cowell punish me like that when I was innocent and had nothing to do with the accident or the adoption? What a Jack Ass!

When I would write thank you letters back to him, Mom (Jan) encouraged me to ask him some questions to try to create some sort of dialogue. So, I have always been a car buff since I was a little kid. Mom told me Grandfather Cowell always got a new Cadillac every year or two. I would ask him about his Cadillacs, eager to hear back. Well, I never heard back. Damn that S.O.B.! I sooooo wanted to know my Cowell grandparents but never did. My mom told me they came to visit one year in Minnesota, but I was too young to remember that. Anyway, I love the fact that I got the last laugh on Grandfather Cowell. You see, even if we were never adopted, and I went through life with my last name as Cowell, I still win, and he loses! That's because I never married (for a variety of reasons), plus I never wanted children. Years later, in the late to mid-nineties, my sister, who was now permanently living in Morocco, and I met up in Washington, DC, as tourists. Aunt Allison lived a day's drive away in Pennsylvania and drove down to meet us. I confronted Aunt Allison on why Grandpa Cowell was so heartless and had nothing to do with me when the circumstances were out of my personal control. Allison replied, "Well when he said something, he meant it and stuck to his guns" or something to that effect. My thought? *What a jerk! I lost out on getting to know both my grandpa and grandma Cowell. I got gipped!*

I never remember being told I was adopted, but yet, I always knew it. I have no memory of my birth parents, only old photos and newspaper articles about them As I say, my adoptive parents were secretive. My biological parents were rarely ever mentioned. Shame on my adoptive parents!

As I grew up and became old enough to observe my surroundings around the age of three or four, I began to see the evil true colors of my new adoptive dad. I can remember two incidents. The first one was when I had a loose baby tooth that was close to falling out but was stubbornly still hanging on. It would not come out. So, my dad tied a piece of string to my tooth and the door handle leading to the garage and *SLAMMED* the door! Out flew my tooth. It scared me. I think that was the wrong way to handle it.

The other incident occurred when my sister and I were waiting in the car while Mom went shopping. My sister was in the front seat, and I was in the back seat. The end result was that my sister pulled on my arm hard enough to dislocate my shoulder accidentally. My sister's version was that I kept harassing her. She became annoyed and began pulling on my arm to get me to stop. My version, as I remember it, I thought was a game, and I was having fun being pulled halfway over the seat.

Later that evening, while we were all having dinner, I started to really complain about the pain. I figured I must have been about four years-old. Dad showed for a second time what a S.O.B. he could be. He kept thinking I was faking it and more or less told me to deal with it. Well, I kept complaining, and *FINALLY,* Dad took me to the emergency room. Sure enough, the hospital determined that my shoulder was dislocated. Dad was proven *WRONG*, and I came home in a sling that night. I now always think of him as A**HOLE DAD. He gets an *F minus* at fatherhood. Read on to see why I came to that conclusion.

Chapter 3

Destination Denver, Difficult Times, and Bullies

In 1964, my father was transferred to Denver, Colorado, with Armco Steel. I was five when we moved there. That's where I spent the next fifty-four years of my life. I recollect very few happy times during that long period of my life.

Now, living in Denver in another house in a new city, life seemed different. We had moved into a relatively new house in a neighborhood that was underway and getting established. There were a lot of parcels of land for sale and open fields. Since then, it has become all built up, and all the fields have disappeared; there is no open space left for miles in every direction. Denver was not as big in 1964 as it is today.

Our house was two-story and painted white. It was not anything special—just your typical middle-class two-story house. There was nothing really impressive about it. I think we all missed our Minnesota home. I know my dad really missed it, as he used to talk about it fondly every now and again.

Upon moving to Denver, life became even more challenging for me. I grew up in an extremely dysfunctional family. I attribute it mainly to my parents and their inability to know how to be good parents. Both were extremely controlling. Mom was very bad about this even up till the last day of her life. She was much worse than my father.

I became a bully magnet. It was like I had a tattoo on my forehead that read "Bully Me." Maybe since I've always been a sensitive person, it showed through and made me look vulnerable. Bullying has followed me throughout eighty-five percent of my life. When I look back, Denver seems to be the birthplace where it all began. In recent years, the bullying seems to have finally stopped. The bullying continued past post-college life and carried over into my professional working life from certain friends, co-workers, and a supervisor. In one particular case, a manager of an office I worked in embarrassed me in front of my co-workers.

Even my dad bullied me from time to time. Long story short, my dad was a *put-down artist* (a phrase my mom coined to describe him), always finding fault with me. He was a difficult man to get along with. He had always thought his opinion on things was right, and if you disagreed with him, you were wrong.

The next round of bullies lived in my neighborhood. There were five main ones. I was really scared of four of them. Growing up, there was a neighborhood kid I was best friends with. I will call him Jack. We got along great till around eighth grade, and around that time, he turned on me and became abrasive. What brought on this sudden change, I will never know. I do know that he started hanging tight with another person from school who always hated and hassled me from grade school through my senior year of high school. He will be referred to as Larry, and I will get to him later.

Then there was a kid named Marty. I must have been in first grade, about six years old. He was my same age. I can remember that sometimes he would act like my friend, and other times he would be my enemy. One summer evening, I was standing in front of his house, and for some reason, he just took his fist and hit me in the mouth, knocking out a lower front baby tooth. I have no recollection of what provoked him. However, I remember running right home after that, probably crying, and told my parents what had happened. They were not going to do anything. But my mother pushed my dad to talk to Marty's father after we ate dinner. When my dad returned home, Marty's father defended his son and told my dad, "Teach your kid how to fight."

The next kid, I will call Keith. He was known as the kid in the neighborhood who was always up to no good. He was always getting into trouble and sometimes wanted to be my friend off and on growing up. He was one of the people who bullied me frequently. His moment of glory came when he set on fire a new house under construction in our neighborhood. The house was in the framing stages but also was partially completed on the main part of the house. Keith happened to be in the framed part of the garage. He told me he was playing with matches, and a fire started; as the story goes, it started to get out of hand. There happened to be a can of turpentine nearby. I assumed he panicked as he dumped the turpentine on the fire to try to put it out. That's when the house started to go up in flames. Mainly, the garage was damaged, thanks to the fire department that put the fire out. The garage would need to be rebuilt, and I'm sure other parts of the house got damaged. It was not a total loss. I'm sure the construction workers were unhappy after all their hard work had to be redone.

    I think Keith had a hard time making friends, and I occasionally made the mistake of loosely being friends with him. One time he bullied me very badly. It was the summer. I was the only one home. I may have been in third grade. I think we were racing skateboards around in our garage. He began to hassle me, and now, at this point, I tried to get away from him and go inside. I put the garage door down by hand and tried to enter the house. Well, the damn door was locked. My mom apparently locked the door, so I had no way of getting in. We had a window on the side of the garage. Keith kept looking in to see where I was. Now, I was a sitting duck, getting even more scared as I had to sit in the garage, waiting for Mom to come home as Keith was up to plotting something to get to me. Keith figured out a brilliant way that caught me completely off guard. I thought up until this moment, I was relatively safe. Then, the little bastard turned on our outside faucet, where there was a hose attached. Keith opened the garage door about three feet with one hand and, in the other, sprayed the hose at me. He got me all wet, along with getting some of the unpainted drywall in the garage wet. He created watermarks. I was crying to his delight with no way out. It didn't last too long, but when Mom got home, I was so mad at her for leaving the door locked as I explained what I had endured. She apologized for locking the door, and that's about all she said.

    When Keith was friendly with me, he became a bad influence on me. He talked me into going over to a neighbor's house while they were on vacation. He coached me into helping him create mud and then using all four of our hands to place muddy handprints all over their white garage door. In another incident during a summer night after it was dark, there was a big deep pothole in front of his house. It had a couple of those road construction sawhorses that were painted with reflective white and orange diagonal stripes with a yellow blinking light on top to note caution. I watched Keith move both sawhorses to the side of the street where the road was not damaged to have cars avoid the sawhorses and drive into the big pothole. That scared me as I knew that wasn't right, so I went home as I did not want to be around if a car got damaged running through the pothole. I don't know if any cars got damaged. But this was the typical thing Keith was always up to. Another time he wanted me to go with him on our bikes around Halloween. He wanted to take people's pumpkins off their porches and smash them in the street. I felt guilty as I knew what it felt like because that had happened to me on some Halloweens before I learned to put the pumpkins in the window.

The neighborhood was expanding with new construction just past Keith's residence. Next to Keith's home sat a bulldozer for digging foundations. It was left there over the weekend. One summer afternoon, Keith and I were hanging near the bulldozer. Keith noticed they had left the key in it and decided to start it up. I warned him not to do it. He started it up anyway, pulling some levers and then turning the key and shutting the engine down.

Then there was the Flagler family. They had five kids. Two of their boys *really* bullied me verbally. They were the ones that I was most afraid of. I will refer to their trouble-making kids as Poindexter and Joey. Poindexter was the worst of the two. He constantly hassled me at school and in the neighborhood. My mom pushed me to join Cub Scouts. Guess who the Den Mother was? You guessed right if you said Poindexter's mother. Man, I didn't want to be in Cub Scouts to begin with, and having Poindexter's Mother as Den Mother meant I would have to be going to his house for the meetings to earn badges and such.

Once, I was at his house after school for a meeting where we had to complete a task for a merit badge, and Poindexter kept screwing with me. I was not able to complete the task. I finally had to go to Poindexter's Mom to get him to back off. Poindexter was not too happy with me. I even think I left the meeting early due to his bullying.

One evening at our grade school where all the other Cub Scout Packs met, I chose to hang around Poindexter and some other Cub Scouts before the assembly started. We were horsing around in the cafeteria that was connected to the gym. We were all taking turns swinging on the ropes that were used for gym class and landing on an overturned plastic trash can. Well, when my turn came, I went swinging on the rope, and right before I was to land on the trash can, Poindexter kicked it to the side, and I fell hard on to the tile floor damaging my right knee. It hurt! I'm sure Poindexter got a great laugh out of it. Nothing was broken, but for years after that, occasionally, it hurt enough at times I'd have to limp. I quit Cub Scouts within less than two years of participating, mainly because of Poindexter.

Other kids in the neighborhood and at school would pick on me, and I got beat up a lot as a little kid. There are too many other incidents to list, but these really stick out in my memory.

Chapter 4

The Disparaging Father

My adoptive father and I were never very close. All my life, I yearned to have a close relationship with him, but it was never meant to be. He was a difficult man to be around. We had a toxic relationship, and he never took an interest in my interests. Oh, but I admired and wanted to be just like him when I was young. I really wanted him to be my best friend. Sadly, I was in high school when I was old enough to discover his true character.

As an adult, I missed the opportunity to sit down with him and bond over a few beers. I would have loved to have had a good chat over nothing in particular, chewing the fat, talking about life, philosophy, traveling, or whatever came to mind. It would be a deep, memorable conversation. However, that could have never been possible as he was an alcoholic and joined Alcoholics Anonymous when I was in high school. Dad claimed to me that he had a *gene* that *made* him drink. That's a cop-out excuse and a refusal to take self-responsibility for drinking. No one held a gun to his head, *forcing him to drink*. The choice to drink was my dad's.

Mom told me as an adult that Dad adored us as little kids. Unfortunately, my sister and I created a faux pas: we grew up and became adults. Mom shared another piece of information about him with me. She had admitted to me that as we were growing up, she recognized he never did anything with us. When she confronted him about it, he responded, "When they get old enough to do the things I want to do, then I will do things with them."

He constantly found fault with me and stripped me of my self-confidence when I was around him. Then, when I was forty-five, he cut off all communication with me and my sister for the last twelve years of his life.

During the sixties, long hair came into fashion for men and boys. In first grade, circa 1965, I had a buzz cut, courtesy of my dad. Meanwhile, most boys had grown out their hair, ears showing the all-American classic look, while I was the odd man out. I asked Dad if I could grow my hair out in second grade to fit in. Surprisingly, he agreed.

By the time third grade rolled around, most boys had long hair, following the Beatle craze. Not me. I was *FORBIDDEN* to have long hair, and it drove me crazy as I wanted it so *badly*. My dad even refused to let me have sideburns. He made sure they stopped right at eye level, military-like. Now for the *second time*, I was the odd man out. I was among the *very few boys* who did not have long hair, and we stood out. I was not even allowed to have hair over the tops of my ears.

At dinner one night while I was in fifth grade, Dad had an outlandish idea. I had my hair grown out with the All-American look, and he started ragging on me again over dinner and how he thought my hair was too long. It was circa 1968, and so my dad asked me if he could cut my hair after dinner. Again, I was afraid to stand up to him and say no. However, he was my dad, and I *trusted* him. *BIG MISTAKE!*

Once dinner was over, we went to the basement, and I sat on a stool. Dad got out the electric clippers. Only a small mirror was hanging on the wall a few feet away to my right. I was putting 100% trust in him but couldn't see what he was doing. Mom came down to check on me. She was horrified! That's when I became scared and alarmed. I jumped off the stool and leaped over to the nearby mirror on the wall. I now had a buzz cut in front. I don't think Dad had even gotten to the rest of my head. Mom became furious at my dad, and so did I. I was so embarrassed and again felt humiliated. The following day, we took our individual and class photos. I looked like a complete fool! Dad loved the buzz-cut look. As an adult, I asked my mom once why she let this happen, and she said, "Your dad was drunk when he did it." Screw you, Dad!

Ah, but when my parents divorced when I was a teenager, my mom allowed me to grow long hair. I grew it down to my shoulders. When Dad picked me up on weekends, he often insulted me and said I looked like a girl. I really believe my dad's defiant stance against long hair had a huge psychological effect on me. During my working life, unfortunately, I had to maintain short hair.

Around the age of fifty-five, I gained more self-confidence. That's when I decided to be my true *self* and stop being pretentious, who I am not, appearance-wise. This is when I stopped seeking approval by doing what others thought I should do. I now decided to look how I've wanted to for a long time. At that time, I decided to grow my ponytail that I had wanted since the late 1980s after having seen a TV show where a character wore a ponytail with a business suit. I thought it looked trendy. Nowadays, ponytails may not be in style for men; however, I don't care. I'm doing what I want and don't need to conform to the cookie-cutter look of men who wear short hair. At one point, I let my hair grow halfway down my back. I loved it, and I'm loving every minute of it, *BABY!*

For most of my life, I have viewed my dad as an evil man. It was at the dinner table where he held court. It was *Dad* who determined the topic of conversation each night. I knew he would spar with one of us and make trouble at each meal. Some of the things that *really* stand out in my memory are as follows.

I have no memory of what prompted this ill-advised move by my dad, but he did it to my sister, as well, when we lived in Minnesota. Let me preface this: I was raised to eat everything on my plate and not leave the table until I had done so. *No exceptions!* Taking a bite just to try it was unacceptable. All I can think of that prompted this incident was that I did not like what was served for dinner, and I would not eat it. I must have been six or seven. While I still had much food on my plate, Dad reached over, picked up my glass of milk, and proceeded to pour it all over the food, and made me eat *everything on my plate.*

I didn't always speak clearly as a kid—or so my dad thought. One night at the dinner table, he started to pick on me, saying that I mumbled my words and wasn't speaking clearly enough. He went on to explain to me about King George VI of England, who spoke with a stutter. He'd had pebbles placed in his mouth to try to learn to speak correctly. So, you know what that S.O.B. Dad of mine made me do? He made me get up from the table, go out to the gutter in the street, pick up a handful of pebbles, and bring them back to the table. He then instructed me to put them all in my mouth and forced me to talk (all while my mom, sister, and he were eating their meals). After a while, my dad let me spit them out and told me to talk some more. While it's possible he thought I might be talking more clearly, it was an idiotic and humiliating thing to make me go through. I was in fear this whole time and probably wanted to cry. I did not try to resist by saying no to my dad for fear of the consequences. As you can ascertain, I was in fear of my dad quite often while growing up.

On one summer day during lunch, another incident of abuse occurred. He started off on another put-down of me. I was maybe ten. He told me of a gift he had bought me and then decided not to give it to me because I never finished anything. WTF? *Why would he even tell me he bought me something if he was not going to give it to me?* That was hurtful. He made me feel I was not worthy of this gift because of a fault of mine. It would have been better if he had never mentioned it. To this day, I have no idea what he bought. He never told me nor did he give it to me.

When I was nearing the end of my grade school years or starting junior high school, my mother brought home our first cat she had gotten from a friend who was giving away a litter of cats. We already had a poodle named Jocko. Although I like dogs, I really love cats. Cats are my favorite animals in the entire world. Mom named the cat Tommy after Tom and Jerry. About two years later, Mom wanted to get another cat. This time, I asked if it could be my cat. She agreed. So, we went down to the Dumb Friend's League, and I think I picked out the new cat. He was a tuxedo cat with a black upper body and white chest, belly, and paws. My Dad was not happy. Mom named him Jerry, but it didn't seem to suit him. We were at a loss for names. To try to appease my dad, she named our second cat Boots. When Dad was a kid, he had a similar-looking cat named Boots. Our new cat responded well when we called him Boots. I always called him Bootsy. Over the course of his life, we became very tight. He slept on my bed at night. Boots knew when I was down and would come to comfort me. He did so many funny things that made me love him even more. Our bond was very strong.

Then one night at the dinner table, court was now in session *again*. I was still in junior high. Dad went off on one of his rants again. I have no idea what got into his head. Maybe Dad was just getting sick of having three animals in the house, or maybe he was drunk again; who knows? During dinner, as I remember it, Dad gave me an ultimatum. He gave me a choice of which cat would have to be put to sleep. He said he was going to make me watch as the vet gave him the lethal dose. I was under *extreme* pressure and terrified. Both cats were still young and in perfect health. I thought long and hard, evaluating which cat it would be. I started to lean toward Tommy as I loved Bootsy more and didn't want to part with him. Still, in deep, serious thought, I realized I didn't want to give either of them up. So, I eventually answered, "Neither cat." My dad backed off then, and I don't remember anything from that meal after that. Was my dad trying to test me, mess with my head, or was he just the mean old bastard who wonderfully played the part so well? Why would a father *even* conceive of such a thought and make his son choose? That was just plain mean!

If this sounds like my dad was always picking on me, my sister got it worse than I ever did. My dad aimed the majority of his toxic lectures toward my sister at the dinner table. While growing up in Denver, I can always remember my dad picking a fight with my sister night after night. Forget any fun civil conversation amongst the family. My sister was usually the target. I have always felt very sorry for my sister as she had to endure ninety-five percent of those brutal lectures. My dad was not kind to her and sometimes would bring her to tears. There is one particular incident that really stands out in my mind. When I was in grade school, I didn't know what my sister did to deserve this. Soon after dinner started, my dad became angry with my sister and ordered her to get up and leave the table before she could really eat anything from her plate and made her spend the rest of the night sleeping in the bathtub in her *clothes!* I felt so sorry for her. That was heartless, and it really bothered me when that side of my dad showed through. Later in the evening, I sneaked her some food. I was *mad* at Dad that night! That was totally uncalled for.

His meanness continued with me. Terrible memories also occurred when we played golf. Remember earlier when I mentioned that Mom told me what Dad said about not wanting to do things with us until we could partake in his interests. Dad was obsessed with golf. He played every Saturday and Sunday. I think he did it partially to get away from my mom. He had me to start playing golf in grade school. By the time I was in junior high school, I was decent enough to play the adult course. I was not that good, and every time I hit a lousy shot, Dad would tell me what I needed to correct. It was like having a golf lesson after every shot. His constant berating tore down any confidence I may have had in playing golf. I knew if I did not hit the ball properly, a lecture would come. Dad took all the fun out of playing golf.

One afternoon, when I was still a kid, around the age of nine or ten, we were winding up our game when we reached the ninth hole. I teed off and the ball may have only traveled twenty to thirty yards. I had been hitting the ball badly all day, and I didn't really want to be there to begin with. Dad started to lose his cool from all my foul shots. When I got ready to hit my second shot, he came over. I could see he was angry and frustrated with me. He knelt before me, grabbed my hands, and showed me the grip to have on the club. He told me to keep my head down with my eye on the ball. He showed me how to take the swing and a few other things like my stance, where to point my feet, etc. I was scared and got really nervous because he told me close to ten things to remember. So, I took the swing, and the ball didn't go far. Then Dad yelled at me. "Why didn't you do what I told you to do?" Well, how could I when he made me nervous. I was under a lot of pressure to hit the *perfect shot*. He had given me too much to think about, and I felt intimidated. I tried my best, wanting to hit the perfect shot, but fear and nervousness set in. I wanted to please him, but I felt humiliated *again!*

These hideous memories continued. In grade school, Dad reached another boiling point of anger once again at the dinner table. For some reason, Dad was mad at my sister and me. He chose to punish us together. He had us get up from the table and stand beside the basement door. He walked over and suddenly knocked our heads together *hard*. It hurt, and you could hear the unmistakable sound of the two skulls when they hit. He knocked them together hard enough that he could possibly have cracked our skulls. In fact, after it happened, I wondered if I had a cracked skull. My sister said he did this to us thrice while growing up. Luckily, our skulls never cracked, but they could have. This was typical behavior from Dad. It was just another dinner with Dad losing his cool. Move along; nothing to see here.

Post college, I once went to visit him in Florida. This time he was seeing a psychiatrist, which shocked me because all the time I was growing up, he was putting them down and referring to them as *Shrinks*. I went along to an appointment with him and waited in the waiting room while he was in session. Near the end of his appointment, they asked me to come in. Dad was very calm, congenial, and friendly. It was weird and unnatural to see him so open and calm. I was pleasantly surprised. He seemed sincere in whatever he was trying to work out. Then he told me, "What you have to say is important." *Really?* I thought. This seemed odd as he had never seemed concerned before. Suddenly, I felt as if he had changed. I felt positive like a breakthrough in our relationship had occurred. Maybe we could bond, and he was willing to hear what I said. I could honestly tell him how painfully and emotionally he had abused me.

While I was in his therapist's office, Dad told me what I had to say was *important*. After I flew home, I remembered what Dad had told me in his therapist's office. If what I had to say was important, I thought this presented an opportune time for me to write an assertive letter pointing out how he had hurt me and the errors of his ways over the years. Based on what seemed to be a nicer new Dad, I thought I might get an apology or at least an explanation of why he had always been a jerk. Boy, did I miss the mark. He wrote back, saying, "That was then, and this is now. I can't be held responsible for what happened back then." Whoa, he was showing his true colors once again. He wouldn't man up and own his past poor behavior. It seemed Dad was still the same old Dad I had always known; just when I thought he was working on himself for improvement, he let me down again.

Fast forward to when I was around the age of thirty-seven. Dad was traveling across the country, and he stopped by for a few days for a quick visit. I had not seen him in a number of years. The first few hours were great seeing him, and we got along well. Then, he fell back into his verbally abusive ways. At this point, I knew the rest of our visit would not go well. It seems this always happened every time we had not seen each other for a long time.

Meanwhile, we were sitting in my finished basement, about ten feet separating us. It doubled as my family room. Somehow, the conversation turned into another one of his stupid lectures, cutting me down about something. I sat there, as usual, just listening as I always had, taking his guff and repeating "Yeah" every so often so as not to cause confrontation even though I disagreed with him. Then, suddenly, it dawned on me. *This is my house, DAMN IT! I'm an adult and no longer have to take this crap!* As kids, he used to tell us, "My house, my rules." Now, the situation had flipped. *This time, we were on my turf!*

I now had confidence in myself. I stood up to him. I started disagreeing with him. I began telling him I thought he was wrong. I no longer feared him. From there, the conversation went downhill and turned into a shouting match because he really got pissed off that I disagreed with him. Now, it was really starting to get out of hand. He stood up and was very red in the face; spittle flew out from between his lips. He continued to yell at me. Then I stood up. I was starting to get the feeling that he might physically strike me. I needed to be ready. I was not going to back down! I had had enough of his crap over a lifetime. As I stood, I had my left arm down by my side with my fist clenched. I was ready to block any swing he may have taken at me. I don't remember what happened after that, but he must have ended the conversation and backed down. We left for dinner after that.

On the way to dinner, I brought up two issues I was having trouble with in my life. I was unable to find a long-term relationship with a woman, and the other was that I still couldn't find the right job for which I was a good fit. On the first issue regarding women, he told me that I'd never be able to find the right woman until I found one that was just as sick as me. My sister told me he said the same thing about me to her. Dad was implying I would have to find someone who had OCD, similar depression issues, and all the other problems I was dealing with. *Where did Dad learn this great psychology to know what my romance problem was and that he knew the answer?* I thought facetiously. *Way to go, Dad; you just chipped away at my self-esteem again, letting me know how deeply flawed I am.* He did not give any positive suggestions. That was the kind of stuff I had to deal with growing up that was continuing through adulthood.

On the second issue, he told me the reason I couldn't find the right job was that I kept getting the same type of job. *WHAT?* He knew that I had been a rental car agent, an insurance adjuster, and had worked at a credit union. I'm not sure if he knew the variety of other jobs I had beyond those. So, how would he conclude they were similar types of jobs? This really annoyed me as I wanted to know what he meant because it obviously did not make any sense. So, I pressed him to clarify. Once seated at our table in the restaurant, he was dancing around the answer and not really answering my question, which made me want to press him harder. At this time, he began to make a scene by raising his voice, explaining that he was not going to tell me, and he didn't want to talk about it anymore. I had never seen him cave like that. Meanwhile, I remained calm as Dad started to draw attention from the other patrons to our table. Dad was embarrassing me. When we returned home, the rest of the evening remained awkward. We watched some TV in silence till we both went to bed.

When his visit was over and he left, I noticed the condition in which he left my guest bathroom. He had thrown all the towels on the floor, as you do in a hotel when you want the maid to replace them. It wasn't just the bath towel but a hand towel, as well. That angered me. He totally disrespected me after I was nice enough to let him stay in my home.

The next time Dad came through town, I told him he could not stay with me and would have to stay in a hotel. Even on that visit when he stayed in a hotel, after the first three hours, we started getting into it again. We would quickly get on each other's nerves. It became apparent now that we would never have a positive relationship.

There are many similar stories that I could go into over the course of my life, but they all have the same theme. I've just mentioned the ones that are really burned into my memory. Dad left indelible, permanent, and emotional scars that will remain with me until I'm dead. He left me with few positive memories. Damn, he was a crappy parent.

Chapter 5

Starting School and Coping with Additional Bullies

It was circa 1965 or thereabouts. I was a hyper child and am still a bit hyper today. Sometimes, as an adult, I find it hard to sit still. I even toss and turn every night quite often that my sheets and blankets are in different directions in the morning.

My schooling began at Greenwood Elementary. I would remain there for the next eight years. My kindergarten teacher was a bit crusty; I don't think she liked me. I believe my hyperactivity annoyed her.

I guess I became a problem, and she informed my mom. She was sure I had brain damage. That led to Mom taking me to a medical clinic where they attached a bunch of electrodes to my head and tested my brain to see if I had brain damage. The results *must* have come back negative as nothing came from that.

My first-grade teacher had a very distinctive and pronounced feature about her appearance that I had never seen on *any* woman before, and it baffled me. Her facial hair above her upper lip was very black and hairy. On the first day of class, she showed us around, explaining where to hang our coats in the hallway and where to put our packed lunches if brought from home. She then gathered the boys and showed us the boys' bathroom, which was directly across the hall from our classroom. Then she asked, "Are there any questions?" I raised my hand, and she called on me. I responded very innocently and asked, "Why do you have a mustache?" as I was really perplexed. Well, that sealed my fate with her for the rest of the school year. I could see that after I asked that question, I threw her for a loop. The look on her face was one of anger. I don't remember what she said, but she must have been very embarrassed. However, she was not embarrassed enough to take care of her appearance problem, as she never got rid of her mustache. To this day, I have never ever seen a woman before or since with that much facial hair above her upper lip. She was engaged to be married, surprisingly, as I found her to be an unattractive woman, facial hair notwithstanding. I never liked her, and I'm sure the feeling was mutual.

During that same school year, I had the mindset not to take first grade that seriously. Not that I was cocky or had an attitude, but this was the first year of my schooling. Being so young, I didn't realize the fun of my youth was over, and I'd hit the hard reality of now I'm going to have to learn things and have homework to do till the day I graduated college. For example, I remember we were instructed to take a rectangular piece of paper and fold it into a square. Then, unfold it, and the creases created four boxes. I don't remember what the assignment was, but I didn't do it. Instead, I took a crayon and scribbled drawings in each box and handed it in. During that same year, I had the buzz cut. For some stupid reason, perhaps on a dare, I took some scissors and cut ¾ of an inch of my grown-out mini bangs in the center of my forehead. I remember the teacher got mad and scolded me for it.

As a result of not taking first grade seriously, no doubt I failed and had to repeat it. The following year in my new first-grade class, *I got it*. Now, I understood I was there to be taught.

School has always been tough for me. Giving it my best, I always was a C student all the way through college. I do have learning disabilities. I have dyslexia; I cannot memorize, which always made it hard to study for tests, and I could never understand fractions. To this day, I have difficulty with how fractions work. In all honesty, algebra makes more sense to me, and I understand it better than fractions. I never did too well with algebra either, but it seemed easier to interpret solving algebra problems than dealing with those stupid fractions.

By the third grade, I was first taken out of the regular classroom for not being up to speed with the regular students. I, along with Keith, my on-and-off again friend and bully, were singled out. We went one hour a day to be taught remedial education at a slower pace than the other kids.

During my early school years, I was picked on. I strongly believe my last name, Duckworth, was a big motivator. It didn't help that I've always been sensitive, which probably made me a bully magnet because the bullies knew they could get to me.

I went to school with the same people from grade school to being a senior in high school. I had to put up with a lot of teasing and getting into fights. Over the course of those years, I would be called Ducky, "Fuckworth" and Duck Bill (as in Duck Bill platypus). "How much is a duck worth?" It was not fun, I tell you.

Nothing bothered me more than being called DUCKY. That was the term I was called mostly, and it still emotionally hurts if I'm called that today. It makes me wonder if I would not have been teased as much if my last name remained Cowell. It would be pretty hard to make fun of that name. I felt I had been cursed with the Duckworth name and having Bill in front of it made it worse—just my luck of coincidence. It would have been better if I were named Pete. It would be pretty hard to make fun of those two names put together: Pete Duckworth.

Then came fourth grade. I was taken out of the normal classroom environment by recommendations of my school and put in what was *supposed to be* "slow class." It was off the school grounds but still within the school district. What a mistake and joke that was. I would be picked up in front of my house every morning around 10 a.m. by a tiny school bus. The bus would pick up other kids at their houses from all over the school district. We were all in the same boat. We arrived at the *"Schoolhouse,"* which was actually a small red brick one-story house. It had been converted into a schoolhouse. As you entered, it had only two large rooms on either side of the front door. There was a staircase leading downstairs across from the entrance of the front door that led to some offices. The large room to the left had a blackboard and some desks. The large room to the right contained a foosball table. Only approximately ten students and I attended this so-called *slow class*.

The funny thing is, as it turned out, around four flunky teachers didn't take the time or were not interested in teaching. They were more suited as chaperones than teachers. We had free reign to wander off and do anything we wanted. Essentially, the other kids and I just goofed off for the whole school year. One of the ways we wasted time was at a baseball field down the hill behind the house. We would hang out in the dugouts and look for cigarette butts that were still salvageable but had not been fully smoked. We would light those babies up, smoke what we could of them, and then look for more. There was a convenience store nearby where we often frequented to buy candy and bubble gum. Across from the *schoolhouse* was some sort of construction. There had been an excavation dug where dirt mounds had been piled high that we played on.

At one point during the school year, the teachers, if you could even call them that, must have gotten in trouble as one day we arrived at the *schoolhouse*. They laid down the law. They informed us that they would now be teaching us in a classroom format. Well, that didn't last too long. Not even a full school day. The next day, we were back to our routine of goofing off, and the teachers couldn't care less. I don't know how, but I passed the fourth grade.

In addition to my fourth-grade year, I was sent to my first psychiatrist. Many more would follow over the course of my life. I was put on some type of drug to calm me down from my hyperactivity. I don't know if it was Ritalin or not. In my opinion, seeing this psychiatrist was a total waste of time. I remember going to his office weekly. I would work on putting together a plastic model. I don't remember him ever talking to me much while in his office. I do remember once walking with him to a nearby pie shop. We had some pie while he talked to me, probably trying to pick my brain and see what made me tick. I only saw him during that fourth-grade school year. I think the school engineered the motive for me to see him. Years later in my adult life, I confronted Mom about why I was sent to this so-called *slow class* and told her I learned nothing as it was a waste of time. She told me then that the school recommended I attend the so-called *slow class*.

The following year I was back at Greenwood Elementary, starting fifth grade. I had a teacher who seemed to like me, and I was deemed by the class as the *teacher's pet*. The teacher and I got along well, but I wouldn't say I was the *teacher's pet*. That year in school, three things stood out in my memory. First, this was the same year my dad gave me a buzz cut after dinner while drunk. I found that traumatizing to face my classmates. The second was when we switched classes to another room across the hall with another teacher for a specific subject. Keith was up to no good again, and

I became the focus of his mean trick. He asked me to sign a blank piece of paper. At the time, I questioned it, but he said he just wanted my signature. I didn't trust him but thought, *okay, kinda weird,* but didn't think much of it beyond that. Come to find out later that day, on the blank piece of paper, Keith had written a nasty/hateful note to the teacher because I don't think he liked her. Well, when I found out, I was horrified because I liked her. I sought out that teacher and apologized profusely and explained that I would never do such a thing. Then I went on to say Keith wrote the letter and tricked me. She was very understanding and didn't think it was from me. I think she had a feeling it came from Keith. The third thing that year was that I was selected to assist in teaching second or third-graders. At the time, I felt honored to be selected by my fifth-grade teacher. Once I got much older, I always wondered if I were being put in a slow class situation again. Maybe I was not understanding what was being taught *in my classroom* for those few hours each day, or perhaps it was legitimate, and the teacher saw something in me that could help the younger students. That question will always go unanswered.

Around fifth grade, I had the living daylights scared out of me by another neighborhood bully who was a year ahead of me in school. This kid would always tease me. One afternoon when I was getting on the school bus to come home, this kid must have said something derogatory to me. So, I flipped him off after finally being pushed to the limit by his bullying. That was a huge mistake. He told me that when I got off the bus, he was going to beat me up. His stop was after mine. On the bus ride home, I was sweating bullets. He was bigger than I was. I had to figure out a plan for how to get out of this. I came up with what I *thought* was a brilliant plan. All I would have to do is get off at the bus stop before mine. I watched the kids get off the bus when we reached that stop. I waited till the last possible second as the school bus driver began to close the door. That's when I bolted for the door! When I got up, so did the bully, and the chase was on! I have never before been that scared. I ran as fast as I could. I was filled with fear that I'd be beaten to a pulp. It was like I was trying to win a sprint race. As I ran, I kept looking over my shoulder to keep tabs on the lead I had. At first, I thought I'd have a chance. A perfect analogy would be a lion singling out one gazelle at a watering hole. That single gazelle is now running for its life as it knows it's about to be killed. That's *EXACTLY* how I felt. The bully was gaining on me as I ran and cut through people's yards. I was thinking *if I can just reach our backyard's wooden fence, I can climb over it and be safe.* I had almost made it. Right when I got to the fence, the bully caught up with me. I had just started to climb the fence when he pulled me off, and he started throwing punches. I was losing. There wasn't much that I could do other than scream for Mom. "Mom! Mom!" I yelled over and over. She never came. When the beating was over, I went inside crying and told her, "I had been screaming for you while I was getting beat up." She was very apologetic but said she didn't hear me.

I had gotten beaten up so many times in my neighborhood that Mom asked one nice neighborhood kid who lived nearby and was in high school if he'd keep a lookout for me and come to my rescue if he saw me ever being attacked.

Throughout the course of my life, in college, post-college, leading into my adult life, and even in the workplace, co-workers verbally bullied me. It lasted well through my adult life. I still run into the occasional person or neighbor who verbally attacks me. I have never been able to figure out why bullies were attracted to me. My young life started out hard, putting up with more than the average child had to.

Chapter 6

The Worst Day of My Life

As the days at home wore on and we were growing up as a family of four, there were some good days all in all, but they were few and far between. Things were starting to deteriorate between the relationship my dad had with my sister. For years, he always found fault with her. She would hear about it at the dinner table nightly.

Things finally boiled over during dinner one night. My sister was a junior in high school. It was 1972, and she was just 16. I was probably in seventh grade. This was *the night* that broke the camel's back for my sister, as she had had enough years of being the metaphoric dinner-time punching bag.

During dinner, Dad brought my sister to tears, berating her about something. Approximately halfway through dinner, Sis, by whom I've always referred to her as, spoke up and said she was going to run away. That *shocked* me. What shocked me even more was that without hesitation, Dad reached into his hip pocket, pulled out his wallet, opened it up, extracted a twenty-dollar bill, handed it to her, and said something to the effect of "Good Luck." I immediately spoke up and said, "Dad, you can't do this!" Mom said something to the effect of "You are *both* just being too *STUBBORN!*" Sis got up from the table and walked out the front door. I cannot believe neither of my parents would voluntarily allow her to leave home. She wound up going back east and staying with some relatives for the summer. I don't think either of my parents liked her. My sister has even mentioned to me that she felt like she was the black sheep of the family.

We suddenly became a family of three. Dad now turned his focus of verbal abuse on Mom and me each night at dinner. I could start to sense my parents' marriage was developing cracks. My parents became more argumentative with each other as time went on. Years earlier, when I was still in grade school, Dad started sleeping in the guest room. I thought that was odd, so I asked Mom why, and she said Dad felt that bed was more comfortable. Soon after that, Dad moved all his clothes that were on hangers into my closet. Again, I also found that odd. I asked Mom once again why Dad was doing that, and she said he needed more closet space. I was too young to pick up on what was happening. I bought what my mom was telling me: hook, line, and sinker.

My sister had returned home to finish her senior year in high school. When the next fall came in 1973, she left for college. I was now in eighth grade. Once my sister was out of the house and away at college, the dysfunctional family I had grown up in really started to fall apart. Mom and Dad were not getting along, and Dad traveled more on several business trips a month for years. I found out later in life that he was trying to get away from Mom. One night at the dinner table, my parents were in a heated argument. I had had enough of seeing my parents bicker. Suddenly, without thinking and just reacting to the tension of the moment, I bluntly interrupted. My voice was loud with a touch of anger. "Why don't you guys just get a divorce!" What my dad said next, without hesitation, was, "You know Bill, that may not be such a bad idea." Whoa, that stunned me because what I just blurted out was completely spontaneous. I never once thought he would take me seriously. I was just tired of their arguing.

Months went by, and what was about to happen would be the next big upheaval in my life. One December night, about a week before Christmas, I saw Mom and Dad in the living room having their nightly cocktails before dinner, speaking in a hush, hush manner. I thought it was strange but then thought nothing of it. Dinner that night went off without a hitch. Neither Mom nor I were being bullied by my dad, and there was no arguing at the table that night. Once we finished dinner, Dad suggested we take a drive, and Mom said she would do the dishes. Okay, now something was definitely up. This was far out of the ordinary. We got in Dad's car and drove about a half mile, and Dad just blurted out, "Bill, your mother and I are getting a divorce." Immediately, I was totally caught off guard as I didn't ever think this would happen to *me*. Right after Dad said that, I covered my face with both hands and started to cry. I think I said, "NO!'" or "Oh No!" Now, I realized I was becoming one of *those* people with divorced parents and living in a broken home. Dad drove to a fast-food restaurant, where he bought us each a soda. We sat down and talked it over. I was still stunned and upset but not so much crying now. He did mention one thing; he told me he would have gotten a divorce years earlier but waited till Sis and I grew older. Once home, I was the first to walk into the house. The dishes were done, and Mom had a compassionate look on her face as to how I took the news. Now, that hush, hush conversation between my parents made sense. Dad was informing her that he was going to tell me after dinner. They explained they were going to wait till after Christmas to tell me, but I'm glad they did *before* Christmas. This way, I could really take in and worship the *last* Christmas I ever had as a family. This had become the worst day/night of my entire life. It still remains so today. Even though my dad could be a real ass, I wish we could have stayed a family. I enjoyed the family unit even though it was not ideal. If it were up to me, I would have chosen to live with my dad at the time. Perhaps it could be the father/son bond I wanted or just that I was related to him by blood. My parents had already decided that I would live with my mom.

A few days after Christmas, Dad started to look for another place to live. He let me go with him as he looked at new places. During this troubled time, he was nice to me. He found a place on the other side of town soon after Christmas. He was so anxious to get out of the house that he was living with lawn furniture in his place till he could buy new furniture.

Now, he had become the *weekend Dad*. He picked me up on Friday nights and dropped me off on Sundays. Sometimes, I would be with him while he was buying furniture. I remember one incident that I thought was *very* inappropriate for a kid who was twelve. We went into a furniture store, and a nice saleslady started helping us. She was an attractive woman, around my dad's age. Dad picked out some furniture, and as she was writing up the paperwork, Dad started flirting with her. "Can I buy you something?" he asked the saleslady. At first, she turned him down. "No, really, can I buy you something?" he asked her once again. Naturally, this made me feel very uncomfortable, as it had only been around a month since my parents had split up. He went on to ask her out in front of me. *NOT COOL, DAD!*

Years later, I met an attractive divorced lady briefly. It was in a business setting among other people where it was not appropriate to ask her out. Weeks later, I saw her in the grocery store with her daughter, who must have been around seven years-old. I went over to say hello, and I really wanted to ask her out, but then, suddenly, I thought back to my dad's situation with the saleslady. I was now in my dad's shoes. I did not want to put this lady's daughter in the same awkward place he put me in. I thought asking her out in front of her daughter would be very inappropriate. We made some small talk, and it didn't last long; then I continued with my shopping.

Another time within the first few years of my parents' divorce, Dad took me to a restaurant near downtown Denver. After dinner, we got back in his car. He then said, "I have got to drop these off at this lady's house." As he was saying that, he grabbed a pair of women's nylons from the back seat of his car. *AGAIN, NOT COOL, DAD!* The restaurant just happened to be near this lady's house. I was embarrassed. I did not want to know about my dad's sexual exploits with women. That's private business, and it's *not* to be shared with me. That's just plain poor taste.

Chapter 7

Homelife and the Makings of an Unhappy Childhood

I grew up in the textbook definition of a dysfunctional family. I have often wondered if my biological parents were not killed or if another family had adopted us if my life would have been happier. When I look at my friends' childhoods, they did not seem to have it as bad as Sis and I. I believe my sister would concur. If my sister and I ever complained after one of Dad's dinner-time lectures, I remember him oftentimes yelling, "You live under a Dictatorship! END OF SUBJECT!"

Both parents were extremely controlling, my mom much more so than my dad. They controlled our time with chores and even tried to mold us into what they wanted us to be. They wanted us to like their interests and did not allow us to develop into the independent individuals we wanted. We were not a close physical family. There were no hugs. We rarely had any free time to ourselves. This is why, as an adult, I cherish any free time and now do as I please. I love living a relaxing lifestyle as an adult because of the free time that was stolen from me as a child.

I have a theory on why each parent was controlling. I think Mom grew up in a family where her parents kept the children busy doing things daily. Now, my dad's background was a bit different. He was a juvenile delinquent. He was getting into trouble to the point that my grandfather Duckworth got fed up and sent him off to military school. I think both parents wanted to keep us busy so we wouldn't get into trouble and they could keep an eye on us. Hell, I don't know. I was always really jealous of the other kids who had the freedom that I never had. To be fair, my parents didn't control 100% of my time. Sometimes, I got some individual time, but they controlled about 80% of it.

They were also very strict. I had a bedtime all the way through high school. In grade school through junior high, it went from 7:30 p.m. up to 8:30 p.m. In high school, I had to be in bed by 10 p.m. I remember after my parents divorced, Mom bought me a portable TV for my birthday. I kept it in my bedroom. Even on school nights, having to be in bed by 9 p.m., I used to watch TV, and if Mom heard it, she would tell me to turn it off. I listened intently at a low volume so I could turn it off if I heard her coming. It literally sounds like prison rules. *Lights out at 10 p.m. A little strict, don't you think?*

Mom was always one who was full of energy. She kept busy with projects around the house and in the summer months. Her alarm would go off at 7 a.m. daily, and she'd hit the ground running—fully rested, never groggy. She would then walk down the hallway to our rooms, all chipper, and say, "Rise and shine!" We were *NEVER* permitted to sleep in and had to be down for breakfast around 8 a.m. I tend to be a person who needs more than eight hours of sleep. My mom always had the attitude that whatever worked for her should work for everyone. This included whatever she served for meals. If she liked it, then we *had* to like it.

Mom thoroughly cleaned our two-story, average middle-class home, top to bottom, once a week and made it an all-day project *religiously*. Mom had a cleaning lady that she would pick up every Tuesday morning and drive her home around 5 p.m. She and Mom would clean together as a team, and it would *still* take them both all day to clean to meet Mom's standards. Every week, they would wash all the woodwork, move all the furniture away from the walls, and vacuum behind them. Mom kept our house as if it were a museum. Mom would clean the house again on the weekends till Tuesday rolled around again for the big cleaning. My sister was given many more chores than I was. I remember Sis telling me that she asked Mom why she always had to clean the bathrooms and I did not. Mom's response was, "Because he's a boy, and you're a girl." My sister was given chores to do, one after the other, without ever having a finite list. This would include cleaning the oven and doing all the ironing for the whole family. During the summer months, my sister would get up every Saturday morning at 6 a.m., thinking she could get a head start and be done early because she was usually told to wash all the outside downstairs windows in our house and had to use a ladder to reach the top of the windows. This took extra time as the windows in our house were square windowpanes that were approximately 7 x 7 inches. When my sister was done with all her chores around noon, she thought she would have some free time. Nope. Sis finished up, and there were still a few hours left after lunch. According to my sister, Mom would then say to her, "Now you can do this other job." Mom would usually keep her working until about 3:00-4:00 p.m. in the afternoon.

As for me, I remember some chores I had to do were clipping the grass around the fence in the backyard, sometimes shared between Sis and me. In addition to miscellaneous chores, I had to clean up the dog waste from our dog once a week in the backyard. After the divorce, Mom loved to do yard work. She had a few gardens in our backyard. She would make a *HUGE* mess. Tossing weeds trimming flowers onto the grass. From time to time, she would cut sod to make clearly defined edges around the gardens. Now, guess who had the distinct honor of having to clean up that mess she created? There would usually be three to four big piles of garden waste. I needed to use an old green, heavy, metal wheelbarrow and make several trips to the side of the house, where I had to dump it into a trash can. Let me tell you, boy, that heavy sod was a bearcat to haul away.

After the divorce, when I was older, I had gotten fed up with cleaning up the mess she created summer after summer. So, I started to complain and said in a snotty tone, "You created this mess, *YOU* clean it up!" using the analogy of a little kid dumping out all his Lincoln Logs, playing with them for a while, and then just walking away leaving a mess all over the floor. Then you get called back by the parent and told, "When you are done playing, you have to clean it all up and put the pieces back in the container." *So, Mom, clean up your own damn yardwork mess!* I remember one summer when, in grade school, I was cleaning up yard work, and some neighborhood kids pulled up on their bikes and asked if I wanted to go riding with them, and I said, "I can't. I have to do yard work." God, I hated being a prisoner of my parents, not being able to enjoy the freedom other kids had.

Chapter 8

OCD Prison, A Life Sentence

According to Lokesh Jaral, who wrote the article "What is OCD? What Triggers OCD The Most" for the blog, Deasilex.com, "Obsessive-Compulsive Disorder, OCD, is a mental disorder in which a person's thoughts and behaviors are uncontrollable and persistent, or psychological behaviors that require constant repeating. The OCD cycle begins with a trigger, accompanied by stress-inducing emotions, pictures, or desires, and finally fixation."

I have OCD, and I'm not alone. According to diagnostic interview data from the National Comorbidity Survey Replication (NCS-R), it is estimated that 1.2 US adults (aged 18 or older) had OCD in the past year. Past year prevalence of OCD was higher for females (1.8 %) than for males (0.5%)" (*National Institute of Mental Health*).

This is a difficult chapter for me to write because I will be exposing secrets to people who know me of which they are unaware. This OCD affects me in many ways, although my biggest fear is contamination. As a result, I wash my hands often. For the readers who don't have OCD, you need to understand the stress I live with daily. I will be as transparent as I can, sharing what I feel comfortable exposing. I will omit certain things for fear of extreme embarrassment. I will explain the emotional terror I deal with 24/7/365. First, I need to educate you on how I became afflicted and some facts about OCD.

A major life event usually triggers OCD. To the best of my knowledge, I can trace it back to the divorce of my adopted parents, which devastated me. This OCD is the worst curse of a lifetime that I've been saddled with to this day. There is the old cliché, "I would not wish this on my worst enemy." Well, I have known some real *SOBs* in my life that it would be a pleasure to bestow my OCD issues upon as it causes me pure hell every day. It is inescapable. That's why I refer to it as *OCD Prison*. It is a life-long sentence, and I have been informed by medical personnel that there is *no cure*.

OCD has been around for many centuries before it was given an official name in the 1980s. In the early 20th century, scientists studied this mental illness. It was referred to by several different names, such as "Obsessive neurosis," "Scrupulosity," "Religious melancholy," and "Obsessional illness" (*medstanford.edu*).

Many famous people throughout history have had OCD. To mention just a few notable names are Charles Dickens, David Beckham, Jenifer Love Hewitt, Charlize Theron, and Nikola Tesla. Two famous people who have/had severe cases of OCD, as severe or worse than I have are Howie Mandel and Howard Hughes. Because of Howie's fears of contamination, he won't shake hands. Instead, he opts to do fist bumps. According to an *ABC News 20/20* story by David Muir, November 28, 2009, Howie built a home behind his main house, so he could go live there by himself when his anxiety level got too high. His experiences deal with the same torture as I do daily. In his autobiography, *Here's the Deal: Don't Touch Me,* he goes into his difficulties of living with OCD.

While in high school and early college years, it was not uncommon to sometimes wash my hands up to twenty-five times daily. When I lived in Colorado in the cold winters, I'd sometimes have deep gashes on my knuckles that originated from chapped hands because of washing so often. I spoke to a psychiatrist about other issues I had that I did not know were OCD-related. He informed me I had OCD. *OCD What?* I thought. I had never heard that term before. I never knew anyone else was suffering from the anguish I was dealing with up to that point. I just assumed I was crazy. I thought I was the only soul suffering like this.

Current research shows that OCD is genetically linked. I've been told in order for *me* to have OCD, someone else previously in my blood line had to have had it in order for me to have it. Years ago, I tried to research living blood relatives and ask if they knew of any relative who had OCD, and they said no.

Through research, it has been found that in people who have OCD, the brain is formed differently while in the womb than that of a healthy person. The areas of the brain that are different for people with OCD are the striatum, thalamus, and cortex regions. "They were discovered after scientists from Harvard and MIT compared 600 genes in 592 people with OCD to 560 people without it" ("The Possible OCD Genes").

"According to the article, 'The Possible OCD Genes,' the four genes include:

- NRXNI: A gene that encodes proteins that work in the nervous system as receptors and cell adhesion molecules.
- HTR2A: A gene that effects serotonin receptors and plays a role in perception, mood, and behavior regulation.
- CTTNBP2: A gene that effects neural activation and the formation of synapses.
- REEP3: A gene that affects the formation of neurons and how they function."

On *YouTube* there is a two-minute detailed medical explanation of how the OCD brain is formed differently than a normally-formed brain. The video was produced by Marc Dingman and is titled "2-Minute Neuroscience: Obsessive-Compulsive Disorder (OCD)." This video helps to explain how OCD truly affects a person and makes life difficult for him or her. As of May 2023, Dingman has added a 10-minute video, which covers the same topic. You can access these videos, as well as additional informative videos on other neuroscientific disorders at the following URL: www.youtube.com/@Neuroscientificallychallenged.

In the online article, "The Different Types of OCD," we learn OCD can show up in many forms. It's often thought of as a fear of germs or contamination, but there are more forms. Actually, about 30% of people with OCD fear contamination. Here are just a few other OCD fears:

- fear of harming others
- fear of harming oneself
- fear of sexually harming a child
- fear of your partner leaving you or you having an affair that destroys the relationship
- fear of blasphemy and thinking of God or Jesus in an inappropriate manner
- fear of sexual orientation

Some people feel the need to constantly clean the house when it reasonably does not need to be cleaned. My adoptive mother suffered from that one. In addition, there are people with OCD that are overly obsessed with neatness; everything must line up in an orderly fashion, say on a desk or a shelf. If it is not, they become stressed with anxiety. There are so many types of OCD from which people suffer. I don't suffer from all of them—just a few. But I surely can empathize with the stress and anxiety of people with OCD and what they're going through.

Now that we have a basic understanding of OCD, let's get on to my issues and how I'm affected. I will elaborate further, but first, here is just an overview of some of the *main* things that I'm affected by. Let me present a scenario so you can understand my level of anxiety.

Imagine you're in my shoes and have feces on your hand, and there's no place for you to wash it off and nothing with which to wipe it off. You are forced to keep it on your hand. *Now deal with it.* You become obsessed with wanting to wash your hands. The longer you keep it on your hands, the higher the anxiety builds. Then it snowballs, and you start to freak out. That's how I feel when I've touched something that I feel is contaminated. However, for non-OCD people, it may never occur to them that they've touched something contaminated. Therefore, they feel no compulsion to wash their hands as they don't feel they are dirty. I have a brain that was designed differently.

The next big OCD fear is while driving an automobile. Oftentimes, if I hit a bump or pothole in the road when driving alone, I question if I may have hit a pedestrian or run over an animal. Today I still deal with that fear, but it's drastically been reduced. In addition, I used to be a *checker* but now not so much. In fact, it's pretty nonexistent, but I still have my moments. Being a *checker* means you constantly check on things. In my case, before leaving the house or going to bed at night, I used to double or triple-check that all the doors were locked in case there was a break-in. I used to suffer greatly in terrible fear that if the appliances were not turned off, I'd be afraid of an electrical wall fire that could burn my house to the ground. That one was probably more spurred on by movies when you know something bad is going to happen. (Damn that Hollywood!)

In most cases, OCD usually shows up in people when a child is in his/her teens. As mentioned previously, my major life event that could have triggered my OCD is the divorce of my parents. However, in my opinion, I now believe it happened for another reason and the divorce of my parents may have compounded the problem.

I honestly feel it started for the following reason. Having hit puberty around this time, my testosterone and hormones were raging, and any male can relate back to that time. There was more to this issue that shall remain private, but it brought embarrassment, guilt, and shame. It was a confusing time as I was dealing with a private internal battle that I could not talk to anyone about. As a result, I began to wash my hands often due to the guilt, and that's what I think brought out the OCD in my life. OCD then grew like roots on a tree and morphed into other areas that messed with and plagued my mind. The metaphoric key was thrown away and has never been found. My private day to day battles with OCD demons leave me feeling as if I am living in a fortified steel prison cell with no doors, windows, and no possibility of escape.

Occasionally, I have very severe anxiety attacks. When something comes up randomly that I did not foresee that I deem an *OCD emergency,* suddenly I must think fast on my feet and figure out a way to deal with it. A healthy person could not begin to comprehend what is going through my OCD mind at those times. It causes me to freakout. It might not even affect a healthy person. At times like that my anxiety level can totally flip my world upside down. On two separate occasions, a friend and a cousin had a front-row seat and witnessed my worst-case scenario situations.

I do my best to keep my OCD hidden from friends and the public. Oops, I guess that secret is out now to all who are reading this. Only a limited amount of people knows of my OCD situation. Let me just say for those of you who do not have OCD, I envy you.

My fear of germs can be daunting; therefore, I always carry rubber gloves with me wherever I go. This is an insurance policy for me that gives me needed assurance. For example, If I must use a public restroom, I wear gloves. That way I don't have to wash my hands. Just take off the gloves, toss them in the trash, and I'm good to go. You might ask, "What's the big deal with washing your hands?" Here's the *big deal:* OCD has also been referred to as *The Doubting Disease.* Let me explain. When at home or in public, if I need to wash my hands with soap, as soon as I rinse my hands, I suddenly question, *Did I have soap in my hands? Or did I just rinse my hands off with water only? Since I'm not sure, I had better wash them again just to verify I did have soap on them.* That cycle can repeat itself over and over. Case in point: Before I discovered rubber gloves, I wanted to go to a movie. So, I used the restroom before I left the house and washed my hands with soap, *or did I?* I went round and round rewashing and stayed at the sink for five or ten minutes. Every time I rinsed my hands off with soap, I could not logically decipher if I had soap on them or not. Because of this, I missed the start of the movie due to the dark curse of OCD. What I have figured out to do since when I rinse off my hands with soap, I leave a little bit of the excess soap on my wrist. After I have dried my hands, I look at the soap on my wrist for two reasons:

- First, it confirms *I did have soap on my hands.*
- Second, I try to look at the shape of the soap on my wrist and try to memorize it, much like an inkblot test. So, when I wipe the soap from my wrist, if I have doubts, I think back to the shape of the soap that was on my wrist, and I feel assured. If I have gloves with me and feel I must touch something that I feel may contaminate me, then the gloves protect my clean hands.

Because of my OCD, I loathe showering. Once again while in the shower, I soap up, and the water rinses it off. *The Doubting Disease* kicks in again. Back in the '80s and '90s, I'd often get stuck in the shower for close to an hour just washing over and over because the soap kept rinsing off. Toward the end of the shower, I would keep questioning, *Did I really have soap on my body?* The doubt set in, and I'd have to start all over again. I've cut down the time considerably. On average, now it takes me thirty minutes to complete a shower.

As mentioned earlier, whenever I drive, if I hit a bump or pothole, my mind sometimes goes into the mode, *Jeez! Did I just run over an animal or maybe hit and maim a pedestrian? Even worse, did I kill someone?* About two-thirds of the time, I can shake it off by looking in my rearview mirror. My fear is becoming one of those jerks who commit a hit-and-run. What really bothers me is when I'm driving, I pass an animal or a pedestrian on the side of the road, and at that moment, if I hit a bump/pothole, then I must go back around and retrace my path to verify I did not hit anyone as I could not live with myself if I did.

Here are two examples that actually happened many years ago that caused me fear. The first one makes me laugh when I think back upon it. In high school I was driving my mother's car with my friend sitting shotgun. While driving, I hit a pothole or something, and I immediately swung my neck around to look out the back window to see if anything was in the road. *Nothing there.* So, I kept driving. Still, not feeling comfortable, a few seconds later I repeated the same motion. Again, *nothing.* I still wasn't feeling comfortable as I continued to drive, so I did it a third time. This time my friend looked at me and asked, "What are you looking for?" I began to laugh aloud because I knew by that time my mind was messing with me. But the fact that my friend now looked also made me feel confident nothing had happened. He must have thought I was crazy. I wonder what he was thinking when I kept looking over my shoulder.

The next example is more of a serious nature that freaked me out. *The Blues Brothers* film had just come out. On the spur of the moment, I saw the showtime would soon be starting. It was a twenty-five-minute drive to the theater. I jumped in the car and rushed, keeping within the speed limit. On the way, sure enough, I hit a bump or a pothole. Now, I was in an OCD jam. If I went back to check, then I would miss the start of the movie. If I continued, my conscience would weigh heavily that I may have just killed someone or run over a dog. But because of the fact I was dying to see the movie, I continued on and tried my best to shake it off.

During the entire running time of the movie, I could not enjoy it to its fullest as I was racked with guilt that I may have hurt some living creature.

College and dorm life were bad too. I was often feeling the need to wash my hands. For example, I couldn't touch a stapler if it fell on the floor. (I feel floors are always dirty, even if they've just been washed.) Upon picking up the stapler and putting it back on my desk, a new OCD problem would arise. Now I must wash the stapler because it touched the floor. For the sake of argument, if I accidentally touched the stapler before I washed it—well, now I had a new compelling reason to wash my hands. I was washing my hands because of the transfer of dirt.

I was washing my hands so much in the dorm I was getting teased. I heard a comment from a guy who had just left the community bathroom while I was washing at the sink (I might have been there for three to five minutes), and as he walked down the hallway, he yelled, "There goes that kid washing his hands again." People on my floor were noticing how often I washed my hands and began to question me about it. (At this time, I was still under the impression that I was the only person in the world who had this fear of germs.) Obviously, I wasn't going to admit that, as they wouldn't get it and tease me even more. So, I had to start getting creative. When asked why I was washing my hands so much, I would reply, "I'm working on a science project in my dorm room, and I'm dealing with acid. I'm trying to be sure I get the acid off my hands." *Gee,* I wondered, *what do they think about my working with acid? Acid is dangerous stuff.* I kind of got a mental laugh out of it as I thought it was a pretty good excuse. The hassling of my washing my hands or just the chance the same people on the floor kept seeing me constantly washing caused me to use the bathrooms on other floors, so I would not be recognized.

OCD has caused me problems growing up, post college, including the work environment. I could not tell people that I actually have OCD. They *wouldn't* comprehend it. They had no concept of how difficult my world could be.

In chapter 13, I will go into detail how OCD interfered and caused me problems during my days of employment. During the same time period of working at the insurance company, I was *officially* diagnosed with OCD in the mid-1980s. In a way, it was a relief to know I was not the only person in the world with this horrendous problem. Having now been to many psychiatrists since the fourth grade, I found a new one who could see how bad my OCD was and wanted to know if I wanted to be included in a research study for the Food and Drug Administration (FDA) when they were considering a new drug for approval for OCD called Anafranil. I immediately agreed, as I was looking for anything that might help. Since I was one of the test cases, I was given the drug Anafranil for free. The overseeing doctor was not interested in helping me with my OCD issues. The only thing he was interested in was how the drug was affecting me, and it wasn't helpful. I would go by his office weekly, give him updates, and get a new supply of pills. They made me think more rationally, so I didn't need to wash my hands so often. However, it had some side effects. The biggest one was it would give me cotton mouth when I got nervous. Another one was if I just swallowed the pills without a beverage, after about forty-five minutes, they would give me the most painful heartburn, the dry heaves, and eventually cause me to vomit. It also had some personal side effects that I won't mention. Eventually, years later, I asked to be taken off it due to the side effects as another drug came along.

The FDA eventually approved Anafranil. I had to go back to Anafranil as I found it was the only OCD drug that I responded to. In recent years, the health insurance company I had at the time reduced their financial portion of what they would cover. Now, out of pocket, it would cost $1000 for thirty days' worth of pills. The insurance company used to pay for practically all of it. The health insurance company decided they would only cover $400, and I'd be stuck with paying $600 per month for it. A pharmacist informed me that health insurance companies were trying to get people off older drugs and onto newer ones. I had been on Anafranil since the late 1980s, and I was forced off it around 2018. Another psychiatrist I was seeing put me on an anxiety medication, and it actually works better with no side effects.

When my adopted mother died unexpectedly in 1999, that sent me overboard with my OCD. I was in really bad shape OCD-wise. Relatives picked up on that. A cousin of mine took the lead on her own and did some research. She was able to locate the best person I have ever known who does not have OCD but totally understands the OCD mind and how it works: Carrie, my psychologist. She specializes in OCD. With her help, she has made my life manageable. Prior to meeting Carrie, I was unable to live a normal life as OCD was crippling. She met with me soon after Mom passed and saw how bad I was. The first thing she did was to put me on a *no wash* for seven days to force me to deal with the contamination, and over time, my anxiety level came down. Now obviously, I could not stick to that 100% but tried as best I could. For the most part, she came to help me at my house with OCD issues. She also did cognitive therapy with me. She would make me touch things in my house that I thought were dirty. I would have to keep my hand on the item for ten to fifteen minutes, then resist washing my hands. At first it was extremely difficult, but as the weeks went by with more practice, it got easier. Sometimes things would be difficult, and I'd get a bit mad, but she understood the anxiety I felt. We would also talk through my OCD issues as she helped me.

I had always wanted to get a cat since I grew up with them. However, my OCD prohibited me from getting a pet because of the cat box issue. Well, we looked at solutions, and I found that if I got an electric cat box, I would only have to empty the container once a week on trash night. That worked out beautifully. I kept it in the back room in my basement. I was finally able to get a cat again. She was a one-year-old rescue. I named her Smokey. She was gray with a white belly. Smokey became my rock and the most *important thing* in my life.

Carrie also helped me to travel again after not being able to for the previous six years due to my OCD complications. With Carrie's help, she gave me my life back and made it easier for me to function. I still have some really bad OCD days, but they are fewer and far between. She got me to the point where I was able to move out of Colorado to a warmer climate with no snow. Thank you, Carrie!

As bad as OCD is, I've tried to have a sense of humor about it. For example, when Carrie pushes me to do something uncomfortable, such as certain cleaning in my home, I jokingly try to pull the old Tom Sawyer adage. I'll say, "Hey, why don't you do it for me, then as an OCD person, I can see how a normal person would do it." That way I'd avoid the stress, but, of course, it never worked. By doing it myself and working through the stress is how I get better. On other occasions, when she'd make me do something, I'd say, "Well, according to the *OCD Handbook,* on page 127, paragraph four, line three, it strictly states that people with OCD are not required to do that." She'd laugh, as there is no such handbook. Still another thing I tell people (due to my contamination issues, I have had to throw things out), is that OCD is an expensive sport to play, as if it were optional. Some of the items I've thrown out are books, a new leather jacket, and a camera, and I had to trade in my most favorite car I've ever owned, a 1986 Ford Bronco II, for reasons that the interior got dirty, and I could never get it clean to my satisfaction. OCD told me the interior was still dirty. There have been tons of other items. I can't remember them all, but that's why if you want to play the sport of OCD, you'd better be rich!

My parents could never comprehend what OCD was. They were beyond the reach of trying to educate them to ever understand. They had closed minds when it came to OCD. Dad had told me he grew up in a dysfunctional family, and his way of dealing with things was drinking. Therefore, he always claimed that since I grew up in a dysfunctional family, the way I dealt with it was to develop OCD. That's laughable. He was *so* off the mark. He also told me he'd never understand OCD. He read a few books on it, and he still couldn't grasp it.

Mom never understood it, either. She always thought I was making it up. And if I thought some door handles were contaminated, she would say to me something to the effect of "Not to think/worry about it." Again, laughable. I tried to explain the way I saw some door handles, as if hypothetically speaking, dog feces smeared all over them, and you couldn't wash your hands. Still, she never got it and refused to believe it. She would say things to me when I was planning to go somewhere, and I'd have to prepare for a possible OCD situation that I may encounter while I was out. She would say that I was "preprogramming myself for failure." Other times, she would say, "Just don't worry about it." I would respond to Mom and say, "That's just like saying I have diabetes, and I shouldn't worry about it because it's all in my head." She thought I could just turn it off and say, "Gee, today I don't have diabetes." I continued, "Mom, OCD doesn't work that way." Mom never had a clue as to what OCD was about. I wish Mom lived long enough to meet Carrie. She would have the medical expertise to explain to Mom how OCD works and how it affects the mind.

The thing I find so difficult to communicate with people who don't have OCD is trying to explain how it affects me. I can talk to people and try to explain it to them till I'm blue in the face, but I can't get through to them. They can't comprehend what is simple for them is stressful torture for me. They can't even understand why I have trouble with all my OCD issues. To them, it's not a problem; therefore, *I shouldn't* have a problem. It's so foreign to them. They don't worry about things that can totally ruin my day.

I've been told by others it's only mind over matter. No, *it's not!* They don't know what they're talking about and are uneducated when it comes to OCD. They lack the knowledge that people with an OCD brain is designed differently than non-OCD brains. I've been accused of not taking responsibility and making excuses because I'm not strong enough to deal with my mental issues on my own.

I've even had women stop going out with me when they discovered how bad my OCD was. I once dated a woman who totally flipped out on me because of my OCD. She told me, "Don't call me; don't contact me; don't come by my house; I'm freaked out!" Yeah, like OCD *is my fault.* Sometimes, I must do things differently and get funny looks from strangers. When Covid first broke and people were not sure if it was only an air born virus or if Covid lived on surfaces, some people were afraid to touch things. I was able to relax and could wear gloves in public, and no one looked at me funny for things like pushing a grocery cart.

When the movie *As Good as It Gets* came out, starring Jack Nicholson, who portrayed a character with severe OCD, I went to the theater to see the film. I was curious to see the writer's interpretation. I sat next to a lady and her husband. During the movie, I overheard her say to her husband, "This guy is really crazy." I had to hold back. I almost turned and said to her, "Excuse me, lady, but some of us really do suffer like this from OCD." I wanted to put her in her place; however, I took the high road and just let it go.

Now, I have only scratched the surface of how I am affected by OCD. I've gone over the main points. But there are many more little things that come up daily that I don't foresee. Some of them are large issues, and some are small issues. I use a metaphor to describe it. When I get up in the morning, I don't know what kind of an OCD day I will have. Every day, I must walk through an *OCD minefield,* not knowing if and when I will step on an *OCD landmine.* Somedays go by incident-free, and on other days, OCD can really destroy all my plans for that day. It just depends.

Many times, for Christmas or my birthday, I've wished for an end to OCD. If I could just have one wish, it would be to become OCD-free.

Carrie knows the deep, deep dungeon of OCD hell I live in and has asked me to write a book for people who have OCD to be used as a teaching tool for therapists who specialize in OCD. That way, they learn firsthand from a person who suffers from it as opposed to learning about it from third parties. I'm providing written lyrics I wrote about OCD entitled *Cover It Up.* This is about my real-life experiences of how I've had to cover it up and hide it from people who don't know enough about OCD. They are the ones who give me funny looks, and make snide comments to me.

Cover It Up

You've got to cover it up.
Cover it up,
Cover it up,
You can never let them know.…

You ask yourself what are you going to do?
You panic and you sit and stew.
People take a crazy long stare and wonder who are you?

You sneak around and sneak around.
Never let them know that you are tied and bound.
And it just piles up like a never-ending mound.

You're feeling the stress.
Yet you're doing your best.
Why is God giving me such a test?
Man, it makes me feel so different than all the rest.

You've got to cover it up.
Cover it up,
Cover it up,
You can never let them know....

You've got to cover it up.
Cover it up,
Cover it up,
You can never let them know....

God, you try to share it with someone
And you see that they are stunned.
You pay out too much money to the doctor's fund.

It makes it hard that you have to lie.
When people are around, you wish you could just run and say goodbye.
In a dream and hoping you're high.

God, you know you've had this for oh so long.
And God you're giving everything to be oh so strong.
What you wouldn't give to right this wrong.

People talk behind your back.
They're not understanding what you lack.
They don't know how much you carry and pack.

You've got to cover it up.
Cover it up,
Cover it up,
And you can never let them know....

Cover it up,
Cover it up,
Cover it up….
—Repeat and fade out—

— WILLIAM COWELL DUCKWORTH
   March 31, 2016

Chapter 9

Sides of My Mother
(Dual Personalities, Time Controller and Insensitivity)

Honestly, I'm not that fond of my adopted mother anymore. In fact, I question if she truly loved me based on our rocky relationship over my lifetime. But at the time of her passing, I loved her very much. However, once I healed from the grief, I started looking back objectively and evaluating how she raised me. I became angry and took issue with her. I have mainly negative memories of her and a few positive ones. Our relationship was like a double-edged sword. Mom meant to raise me well, but the way she went about it was wrong, just as my dad had.

We did not always get along well, for the most part, due to her dominant and controlling nature. She would lay guilt trips on me from time to time, bringing my self-worth down to zero.

Mom was a narcissist; she could be evil, mean, and spiteful. Yet, she assisted me with many of my OCD issues, and even though she did not understand it, she made my life easier.

———◆———

After I was informed my parents were divorcing and Christmas passed, I remember helping Dad pack books he wanted to take from the bookshelf in our family room. This was emotionally hard for me. I was witnessing the breakup of our family unit and the finality of it. I was feeling mixed up inside.

A family of four decreased to two. It was just Mom and me now. This is when my relationship began to deteriorate with her. There were always two sides to my mother's personality. Dr. Jekyll and Mrs. Hyde, you could say.

My sister concurs with me. There was the nice public side where everyone thought the world of her. Then at home, she displayed her true authentic side, which was not so likable.

The public side showed through when Mom was out of the house. She rarely revealed her true personality to the public. In all fairness, she didn't always show her dark side at home and could be very nurturing. However, my sister and I often compare notes on how she treated us. We both have horrible memories of how she treated us individually on separate occasions. These were things outside the immediate family no one ever saw.

Some years after my adopted mom's death, I was talking with one of my mom's neighbors, who knew her well, about the frustration I had with her and the two personalities, public and private. Mom's neighbor said something to the effect, "Yes, I saw the two Jans." This validates that it was not *only* my sister and me who witnessed this. I've heard countless times how wonderful Mom was and the praise people would give her. This would come from my college friends, her co-workers, and some of her friends. The most surprising compliments came at Mom's service. Mom had held a job for quite a few years, working at the Colorado State Capitol building in the House Chambers. She eventually got promoted to Chief Assignable Clerk to the elected representatives. This was a place where she loved to work for years while the Colorado Legislature was in session.

At my mom's service, which was held in the Supreme Court Chambers inside the Colorado State Capitol, no one gave a eulogy. I was too upset and shedding some tears to get up and speak about my mom. Even though there was no eulogy, many people came forward to praise her and paint her in a wonderful light. Most notably at the time, Colorado Congressman, The Honorable Scott McInnis, only had nice things to say about her. He had known my mom back when he was in the Colorado State House before he ran as a United States Congressman. He had written wonderful praise about her that he got published in the *Congressional Record*. This is a daily publication in Washington, D.C., for congressional staff, media, and the public to review what had happened in Congress the previous day. At the service, when he finished praising my mom, he gave me a plaque with a framed copy of the first page of the Congressional Record. For years I had it hanging on my wall. However, in therapy after my mom's death,

I dug deep into my past relationship with her and realized that visiting those old memories were not happy ones. They were memories of anger and emotional pain. I've since had to take that plaque off the wall and pack it away. She lacked parenting skills.

While everyone who came to the podium during my mother's service praised her, my sister and I were simultaneously thinking, *that's not the mother I knew.* The Mom I knew was vindictive, spiteful, and extremely controlling to the point that she always had projects or cleaning for us to do and robbed us of any free time for the most part. All that praise that was said about her at her service really caught my sister and me off guard. Later that day, my sister and I discussed the service, and I disagreed, for the most part, with what was being said about Mom, and my sister's reaction was one of surprise as if they were speaking about a stranger.

The controlling, unkind side of my mother would rear its ugly head in daily life at home. I don't know what possessed my mother to be so controlling and demanding, but she was always taking control to *run the show,* so to speak. After the divorce of my adopted parents when I was around twelve or thirteen, my sister left home. It was then I had become the sole focus of my mother's wrath. Mom now ran my life somewhat similar to the way she ran my sister's life when she was living at home. I had little free time to be found. She even tried to control me as an adult when I lived in my own townhouse. My mom seemed to enjoy taking control and telling others what to do. It was built into her nature. As already mentioned, Mom's *LAW* was that it was *VERBOTEN* to *ever* sleep past 8 a.m. My adoptive father's *LAW* was his refusal to allow me to have long hair. These two LAWS by each parent seemed to be their biggest pet peeves in raising children.

Because of the financial settlement after the divorce settlement, Mom had to let the cleaning lady go. So, every weekend that I lived at home throughout my adulthood, I was expected to get up early and help Mom clean the house all weekend. Mom was abnormally obsessed with cleaning house. OCD? Perhaps. She would take eight hours on Saturday to clean the upstairs and eight hours on Sunday to clean the downstairs. I was sometimes required to move the furniture away from the walls to vacuum behind them. This became a long-drawn-out process. You wouldn't think so on the surface, but here's what caused the slowdown, preventing me from just vacuuming and being done with it.

Mom insisted she would have to dust off the furniture that had barely accumulated dust from the week before. In addition, more delay was caused by her need to take a smoke break every hour (incidentally, as she would dust, she always had a cigarette burning in a nearby ashtray). Mom was a chain smoker and smoked three packs of cigarettes a day. I rarely saw her without a cigarette. Sometimes she would forget about that cigarette she had burning in the ashtray on the main floor and be upstairs smoking a second cigarette—two burning cigarettes at the same time on two different floors. This did not happen often, but I did call Mom out when it did happen so that she wouldn't start a fire for being sloppy. Another monkey wrench to slow down the vacuuming was that sometimes, she would decide to call a friend and just chit-chat for a good thirty minutes. Meanwhile, all I could do was sit around waiting for her to get the hell off the phone! We did *not* live in a mansion, just your typical two-story middle-class home.

While still living at home at the time as an adult for OCD reasons, one morning I cleaned my bathroom, and it took maybe thirty minutes (I had to do it in my own OCD way), then I would take a long shower while I dealt with OCD issues. Then I would get dressed and put together and finally go downstairs at 11 a.m. I remember Mom was sitting on the white loveseat in our family room knitting. She was disgusted that it had taken me so long to clean the bathroom, shower, and get put together. She then said to me, "Bill, look how late it is. Just once I wish you would ask me some morning, 'Gee, Mom, what can I do to help you out today?'" *Really?* I thought. That would have *NEVER* occurred to me to say that as she controlled most of my time. Perhaps if she wasn't constantly controlling my time, I might have considered asking how I could help.

Back when my sister and I were kids, Mom had left for a day to go visit a relative in another town. We were glad we had a day to ourselves. Sis and I just relaxed around the house watching TV, enjoying the time we had off from the so-called *warden*. When Mom returned home in the late afternoon, she asked us what we did while she was gone. We told her we didn't do anything more than hang out and take it easy. She was shocked.

She cried out angrily. "You didn't do anything?" She was hoping we'd say we did something constructive. I was nothing but her unpaid employee, so it seemed. When she wanted me to do something, she wanted it done *NOW!* I was supposed to drop everything and come running in like the Calvary to save the day. This usually would occur when, on occasion, I had had some free time on my hands, and I would reply, with a tad of disgust in my voice, and yell back, "Look, the world is not going to come to an end if it's not done right at this moment." I would finish up whatever I was doing and then try to take care of it.

When I was growing up before I hit my teens and we were living in Denver, she had some unusual punishments. I can't remember what I had done, but it was either I sassed back, or I must have spoken profanity. She would sit me in the corner of the kitchen for fifteen minutes after placing hot sauce on my tongue and ensuring I had no relief from water or any other remedy that would quench the burning fire upon my tongue. Another punishment for the same issues is she would clip a clothespin to my tongue and make me sit in the same location for the same amount of time.

One of her other punishments, and again I don't remember what I did, but it happened before I hit my teens, is I would be instructed to go to my mom's bedroom and told to take off my belt and drop my pants, underwear included, and she would whip me hard ten to twelve times. It became such an occurrence that after a while, I had to get creative to protect myself, so I wouldn't get too many whips each time. I'd start yelling "Ow" whether it hurt or not. One time I remember when Mom accidentally missed and whipped me softly. I did get a bit of a mental laugh when I said, "Ow." She immediately replied, "Oh, that didn't hurt." I wasn't that bad of a kid growing up. I never got into deep trouble.

Now that Dad was gone, I also had to mow the yard every weekend, and it would take two hours each time. Sometimes, Mom would fertilize that lawn once or twice a summer when I didn't think it needed it because the grass was already nice and green. As a result, it made the grass grow fast. So fast I would have to mow the yard twice a week. If I didn't, it would clog up the mower, causing the blades to stop. Sometimes I had to cut the grass at a higher setting and then mow it at a lower setting to get the height Mom wanted, which made for four hours. God, I despised mowing a lawn and yard work. I made sure when I moved out that I bought places where yardwork was included in the HOA fees. I avoid yard work whenever possible. It's *worth every penny* to me to hire a service, so I don't have to do it. That's how much I hate it.

In addition, another one of her demands was when it snowed at night and accumulated a few inches before we went to bed, she *insisted* I go out and shovel the walks and driveway. This could even be as late as 10 p.m., which I'm sure was annoying neighbors who were already in bed. When I tried to argue, it was pointless till the snow stopped. Mom insisted *IT HAD TO BE DONE!* Before I went to bed, her excuse was, "It will make it easier for you in the morning when the snow has stopped." I personally subscribe to a different, more logical point of view. I would just let it snow all night and just deal with whatever accumulation there was in the morning. I think Mom just didn't like the idea of the appearance of snow on the driveway and sidewalks. When I had my own apartment and later my townhouse, Mom would call me in the morning while I was sleeping in and *demand* me to come over *immediately* to shovel her property. When I refused, she would yell at me with disgust and try to lay a guilt trip on me by saying, "Well, how would you like it, me being an old woman and shoveling because I may have a heart attack and die? Do you want that?" *Hey, it's not my problem. I've moved out, and she needs to get a neighbor kid to shovel it.* We're talking, on average, two-four inches of snow. It was a rare storm where we sometimes would get three feet of snow with drifts. If that were the case, then that's understandable for me to come over and try to dig her out. However, I would not do it on demand first thing in the morning.

As you can see, Mom was an extremely controlling person. She would always be ordering people around. Post-college, I remember my best friend Tim got married, and Mom and I attended his wedding. At the reception after people had finished their meals and gotten up and started to socialize,

Mom started to assert herself and decided to gather up all the unopened wedding presents. She wanted me to help put them into a corner. Even though she was trying to be helpful, I felt it was not her place to suddenly take charge. I then jumped her case and said she was out of line. Now, if it were my wedding, that would have been fine, but she was a guest at *my* friend's wedding.

Mom was still trying to control me after I moved out. She wanted me to jump and do what she requested on demand, such as the snow shoveling, not taking into consideration my time or plans. Another such incident occurred on a nice summer Sunday morning. I was relaxing in a lawn chair on the balcony of my apartment. I was reading and enjoying the large Sunday paper with all the extra sections. Suddenly, the phone rang. It was Mom demanding right then that I come over and mow the yard. She could not wait to have it mowed later; she wanted it done then! So that ruined the nice time of relaxation of that Sunday morning. Some years later, when I moved to my townhouse, I was suffering from deep depression, and sometimes I would never get out of bed. On other days, I might get up around 4 p.m., which was pretty standard during that troubled time of my life.

During this low spot in my life, Mom would begin calling me from her workplace around nine or ten in the morning. She'd only ask one question: "Are you up yet?"

I'd say no, and we'd end the call. About an hour and a half later, the phone would ring *again,* and I'd answer and hear, "Are you up yet?" she'd ask. I'd say no and hang up. Well, this would continue to go on throughout the day until it got to be around 3 p.m. Mom would call, and by now, she was very angry with me, and I'd hear her speaking in a softer, angry voice through clenched teeth, "*ARE-YOU-UP-YET?*" You see, Mom could not stand the fact that I was not an early riser. It drove her nuts. *What the hell does she care when I'm living in my own house, where I make my own rules, and I am in my late thirties.* She loved to control!

During these depression years of mine, she was trying to help get me out of depression. She found a psychiatrist, so I went to see him a few times. I did not care for him. Our personalities clashed. After about three sessions, he was not helpful. He suggested that for the fourth session, the three of us (Mom, me and he) meet together and talk. When that appointment came, we were all in his office. He stated something to the effect that he could not help me because I was so depressed and that it would be up to me to find the strength to become more positive and dig myself out a bit from my deep depression *before* he could help me. *What the F**K?* Isn't it his job to help people like me get out of my depression? At that point, I just wanted to say *F**K YOU!* And that wasn't all. My mom chimed in and said something like, "Well, Bill, I think he's right." *Whoa, what did she just say? She's siding with him and not with me?* Well, now, I was steaming on the inside. *How could Mom not have sympathy for me and not side with me? How could she side with him?* Boy, when we got to the parking lot, I chewed her out. How could she side with him? She had no idea the deep emotional pain I was going through. How am I who is suffering from such deep depression supposed to bring myself out of it to the point that a psychiatrist can then help me? Isn't the job description of the psychiatrist to help me deal with my problems, get me to a healthy mindset, and to get me out of such deep depression?

That was not the only time Mom sided with others and failed to support me. When I was working as an insurance adjuster, there were times I'd have a really bad day. I'd have insureds and claimants yelling at me over the phone for various reasons based on my claim decisions. Under certain circumstances, there were times we did not owe any money for the claim as it was not our insured's fault for the accident. Sometimes we flat out denied a claim because it was not covered under the policy. These types of days were very common and stressful. I would come home at night and start venting about what a bad day I had. I totally assumed Mom would support me. But, oh no, it went in the opposite direction. She would say things like, "They're not mad at *you;* they're mad at the insurance company." What? Not even! They were mad at me because *I* was the one who personally denied their claim. I would tell my mom how stressful the job was, and she again would *not* be there to support me. She would side with the company and say, "Well, go talk to your supervisor." Oh yeah, that would really help. This wasn't junior high school where you could go talk to your counselor when things got tough. No, if I were to vent to my supervisor about the stress the job was causing me, that would show him I couldn't handle the job and I wasn't right for a promotion down the line.

Once there was a time when I was dealing with a bad breakup with a woman with whom I was deeply in love. She had dumped me, and my mom knew the back story of the relationship. I came home from a personal vacation, arriving from Memphis having just visited Graceland and other music-related fun. I told her this woman was on my mind a lot while on vacation, and my mind was messed up. I wanted to talk about it. All Mom said was, "Just don't think about it," as she proceeded up the stairs to take a nap. *Oh, right, like that is really going to help.* Mom was only there for me twice in my life when she took my side and gave me support and comfort. All the other times, she sided with the *adversaries* in my life. However, near the end of her life, she found another psychiatrist for me that didn't work out. (It's hard to find a good one that is a good fit.) Mom kept telling me, "I'm your number one fan." I took that with sort of a grain of salt, as she had rarely been there when I needed her.

Mom and I argued a lot, which would escalate into shouting matches. During Christmas break one year while in college, we got into such an angry shouting match over what, I cannot remember, but I had had it, and I packed up my things and went back to my place at college and spent the remaining two weeks of the holiday break there. Then, the following year our relationship still wasn't good, and instead of going home for spring break, I remained at college and spent the time at my apartment. I did not want to be around Mom.

Mom occasionally traveled with her boyfriend. She always insisted that I take them to the airport. Her boyfriend had two kids living in the Denver area, and neither of them ever took them to the airport. Again, Mom used me to be on call whenever she demanded it. She could have cared less if it infringed on my time. She made my life hell not on a constant basis but consistently over the years.

I feel it's important to note some other things that you could say were on the evil side that upset me about Mom. I mentioned earlier in this book that there was an understanding that I was not really at liberty to ask questions about my biological parents. I learned things about my biological parents *only* if I asked questions, and then the answers I received were short, concise, and to the point. My adoptive parents would *never* elaborate.

There was a situation that I found unforgivable that my mom did to rid evidence of my biological parents. While in high school during the winter, a cousin was driving from the East Coast to the West Coast. He stopped to see us for a couple of weeks. He was perhaps four years older than I.

Being the control freak my mom was, she came up with a project for my cousin and me to do while he was staying with us. Out of the blue, she decided that the drywall in the garage should be painted white. Mind you, this may have been January or February. I got drafted into the job. Obviously, using a paint roller, you are going to have white dots of splatter over your clothing. Being that it was winter, it was cold in the garage. Therefore, it would require a jacket of some kind. Well, I couldn't wear my good day-to-day down jacket because I'd ruin it. My biological father's flight jacket, which included patches sewn into the leather very similar to what Tom Cruise wore in the *Top Gun* films while riding his motorcycle, was hung in our stairwell where we kept the families' coats. Mom told me to wear that flight jacket. I protested because I knew the paint was going to trash it. But my mom was insistent. I knew it was morally wrong, and the jacket's importance didn't mean as much to me then as it does now. I highly suspect but can't prove that this painting project gave her the perfect opportunity to ruin the jacket, so it would be thrown out. For Mom, that would mean one less reminder of my biological parents.

Mom did not have the compassion I do for animals or the pets we had. I have already mentioned my cat, Boots. She had him put to sleep just because he had random occasions of diarrhea. At these times, Boots would go wherever. Mainly it occurred in my bathtub. Mom used the poor excuse that "his insides were shot." She claimed the vet told her that. (Hogwash!) Boots was still full of energy and not slowing down. She just didn't want to deal with it anymore or care enough about his life. She warned me that if Boots had diarrhea again, she would have him put to sleep. Sure, diarrhea presented a problem, but I'd rather deal with that than have his life taken. Outside of diarrhea, he had no other health problems. Well, Boots had another bout of diarrhea, and *that* was his death warrant. A call from the governor couldn't even stop his fate. Mom was now dead-set on having him put to sleep.

On the day of the appointment to have Boots put to sleep, Mom drove to the vet. I sat in the back, hugging and petting him. *It was dead man walking for sure.* I had never been so upset in my life. I was in my mid-twenties, crying my eyes out. *HE DIDN'T NEED TO DIE!* Once we arrived at the vet, I couldn't go in with my little Boots as I was a total wreck. Mom insisted that I hand Boots over to her. I gave Boots one last goodbye hug, and I accidentally hugged him too tightly, then he coughed. I felt guilty about that. About twenty minutes later, she came out with a cardboard box heavily taped up. It contained Boots. When we got home, I buried him in the backyard. That afternoon, I took a piece of wood and with my old wood burner, I created a headstone for him. While doing it, I called Mom a *MURDERER*. I had never cried like that before for any pet or person I'd known before or since.

She pulled another dirty trick years later after Boots and Tommy had passed on. We had a cat only for about three or four months, and she had him declawed, which I *vehemently* opposed as being inhumane as it hinders a cat from defending itself should the opportunity arise. (To declaw a cat, instead of removing the claws, they de-knuckle them. That is like having the first knuckle of your fingers and toes that contains your nails cut off.) He was a yellow tabby cat. Mom named him *Twenty Carat*, as in 20-carat gold, based on the color of his fur. I called him Tiki for short. His *only* fault was that he was always biting us. Not pleasant, but I chalked it up to his personality and cut him a break. However, Mom had mentioned she didn't care for his biting and threatened to take him to someone's farm where he could live out his life. Time went by, and I forgot all about her threat until one day, I came home from work, and Tiki was *GONE!* I asked Mom where he was, and that's when she informed me she had left Tiki at the farm she mentioned. I'm pretty sure I let into her. She did that behind my back, and I never got to say goodbye to him! I informed her that with Tiki living out in the open, he would not be able to defend himself if he were attacked due to her having Tiki fully declawed. *SHAME ON YOU, MOM!*

The last Christmas I had with my mom was in 1998. On Christmas Eve, we always had a tradition that we got to open one package before we went to bed. That year, Mom selected the package for me to open. After opening it, I was taken aback and shocked at what she had kept from me all those years. Mom gave me a beautiful large satiny type of material that was a print of all the 1948 Olympiads who won metals for each event. It had belonged to my biological father. He was listed for winning a silver medal for swimming the backstroke. I thanked her for this special present. I was also perplexed that I was never made aware that she had this. That meant for the last 39 years, she had kept this a secret from me. *But why?* I thought. I do remember asking my mom why she had kept this from me all these years. I don't remember what she said. That was not fair to me not to let me know.

She also had an intimate relationship with a family friend, which I didn't find out about till after she died. In college, he came over for dinner every Sunday. On Wednesday nights, she had dinner at his place but did not spend the night. His wife was my mom's best friend until she passed. After that, I believe their romantic relationship started. I had known the guy since I was a kid, and he was my psychiatrist up until the time of his death. I don't know why they had to keep it a secret as I was very fond of him and would have approved of the relationship if they had told me. I had suspected they had a relationship going on by some weird *things* that I picked up on. Years later, it clicked, and I put it together. Then a few years after my mom died, a relative confirmed it for me.

Mom also had buried a secret that she was previously married to her college sweetheart before she married my adoptive dad. I found this out from my sister about two years before Mom died. I confronted Mom about it, and she became very angry at me. Apparently, it was an old family secret that they tried to keep buried. The marriage did not end well. I didn't find it anything to be ashamed of. Lots of first marriages don't work out. But again, I was shocked to learn this when I was around thirty-eight. I compared it to a betrayal from my mother. I likened it to her having a previous secret life working for the CIA and never disclosing it to me. I guess what it came down to is that Mom was not honest with me about her true-life story. This was just another side of her where she could be very secretive. Those kinds of things bother me about my parents when I learned more about them after they passed on.

While writing this book, I came across this poem that I had written and forgotten about. I was in the tenth or eleventh grade (circa 1977).

This taps into the pressure and frustration I was feeling about how she controlled me. I was venting. I find it cathartic to write about what I'm really feeling and express it in one of three forms: Lyrically, poetically, or in a written commentary on current events.

Your Puppet

I work for you all day long.
You won't leave me alone.
And when I grab a free minute,
You yank me back and put me to work again.

I do the things you want me to do.
Anything that you say, over and over every day.
I try for a break,
And you put me to work again!

I've had enough!
No more, never again!
I ain't your puppet hanging on a wire.
And you won't have control over me!

You pull my strings.
I bow to your knees.
And then I really resist
But you are calling the shots.
I'm under your command, and I'm working for you again!
No puppet, no puppet, no puppet.
Just leave me alone.
I'm not your puppet, your puppet, your puppet.

— WILLIAM COWELL DUCKWORTH.
　Written circa 1977

Chapter 10

The High School Years/Unlucky in Love

As mentioned in Chapter 3, Jack, my childhood friend, began to really bully me once we entered junior high. One of his favorite things he used to do to me was box my ears with his hands. It was very annoying. It felt almost like my eardrums were bursting upon impact. Things had started to change for the worse, and he was now turning into a part-time jerk. Our friendship began to wane. During the transition of our friendship dissolving, he became best friends with Larry, whom I mentioned in Chapter 3. Larry hated and bullied me. The dislike was mutual.

It was in eighth-grade social studies class when I developed my first crush. This came about because Jack told me the girl who sat in front of him liked me (Not).

Looking back, I think Jack betrayed me as part of his enjoyment of bullying me, as it occurred on a frequent basis. This was about the time our friendship really started to split.

This girl was attractive. So, I believed the lie "hook, line, and sinker". Foolishly, I wrote the typical juvenile love note to see if she actually liked me. To my disadvantage, I had a big cold sore on my lip that was very detractive. In the love note, I included that my cold sore was only temporary. *Now you have to remember,* I'm roughly twelve, and I'm putting it all on the line as I was so naïve back in my youth that I thought the cold sore would be a deal breaker. Obviously, as adults, we know that it is temporary, but try telling that to a twelve-year-old who was trying to put his best foot forward and was very nervous. The love note I wrote said, "Do you like me?" I drew boxes for yes or no. Well, Jack passed her the note. I was excitedly waiting for her response, hoping it was positive. Within three seconds, I heard a bit of a low-level screaming gasp. That was not a good sign. She immediately gave the note back. She checked the NO box. I was crushed. Her responding NO bothered me the rest of the day. That night I was still feeling devastated. I told my mom what had happened at school. I could tell Mom felt sympathy toward me, and she tried to offer comfort by saying, "At least she answered the box." Well, no that didn't help. The girl could have just said a verbal NO and would have had the same result. And so, my disastrous bad luck with women began here. 0-1.

I had taken first-year Spanish in eighth grade. My Spanish teacher had presented to the class an opportunity over the summer to go on a month-long trip deep in the heart of Mexico just north of Mexico City to a little town called Guanajuato. The purpose of the trip would be for the students to be matched up with a family, which would force us to speak Spanish. Sink or swim. While there, we would attend class to learn more Spanish, taught by our teacher, who went on the trip with us. The brass ring bonus of the trip was when we went back to the United States and started school in the fall, we got to skip forward a year in Spanish. The trip cost approximately $450.00, and the year was 1973. I asked my parents if could go on the trip, and they agreed I could. Now you'd think your own parents would pay for the trip, as remember I was around thirteen now, and my birthday was in the spring. Guess what? I had to pay for it out of the money that was left to me by my biological parents. At that time, my grandfather, Grandpa Ducky, was the manager in charge of the trust. My dad had previously spoken to my grandfather about this trip and agreed it would be a great learning experience, which it was. I did not know at the time that Dad and Grandpa Ducky were in agreement. So, my dad said I would have to call my grandfather and put my best foot forward and argue the case of why I should go. Dad told me before I called Grandpa Ducky to present my case well and, "You got to sell yourself." So, I made the call, nervous as I was; I went into detail explaining what a great opportunity it would be for me. When I rested my case, Grandpa Ducky agreed with me and released the funds so I could go. When I became an adult, I found it irritating that I had to pay for it.

During that trip, another attractive female student from another Spanish class from our school in Colorado went with the group. I will call her Sally.

I found her extremely beautiful, far better looking than the girl from my social studies class. I developed my next crush on her. I did my best to befriend her on that trip to Guanajuato without much success, but I was able to get her number. When we got back to Denver, we talked for most of the rest of the summer. I called her every day. I wanted to ask her out but was only around thirteen, three years shy of getting my driver's license. She was not enamored with me as I was of her. She told me I was boring. That comment has always haunted me to this day. As a result, I try not to come across as boring when dating. She also had an uneasy feeling about me, saying if we went out on a date assuming I could drive, she feared I would take her to a deserted wide-open area of land and leave her there. That's not me. I would never think of doing such a thing. Anyway, toward the end of summer, we ceased our communication. 0-2. Incidentally, at our ten-year high school reunion, we walked past each other, and she said, "Hi, Doug." Obviously, I never meant anything to her since she forgot my name. That hurt, as I thought I might be able to reconnect with her as an adult all those years later.

During that same summer between eighth grade and starting school as a freshman at high school, my mother and I were really going at each other's throats, arguing all the time. My guess would be that she was controlling me too much and taking away any spare time that I had. Well, one particular night, late in the evening during a heated argument, as Mom walked up the stairs to go to bed, I had had it with her and my life. I was distraught. What happened next was my first of four attempts at suicide. As Mom ascended the stairs, I made a *B Line* straight for the knife drawer in the kitchen. I pulled the drawer open and grabbed the first steak knife I saw. As I was in the process, my swooping right arm came down in an arch-like motion to stab myself through the heart. Suddenly, I stopped when the tip of the knife came within one centimeter of touching my shirt. *This is going to hurt,* I thought to myself. I chickened out and put the knife back in the drawer. I don't remember if I ever told Mom what happened that night.

By the time I entered high school as a freshman, my friendship with Jack had run its course. The once-tight friendship we had built had come to an end. Larry was in my freshman history class and told me he was going to make my life miserable that semester. To add more salt to the wound, the times I ate in the cafeteria, he verbally hassled me every time I entered. I had no choice but to walk by his table, as it was next to the entrance of the cafeteria. He and his buddies, which sometimes included Jack and Larry, would yell things out like "Oh, there's DUCKY!" or make some derogatory comment as I walked past his table. Now, remember, Larry had been hassling me since second grade. *Why did he hate me so much?*

Larry was not the only bully I had to deal with in high school. Entering my sophomore year, I was still dealing with problems in my life outside of learning and studying. I had another jerk who was a thorn in my side going back to junior high school. There he sat in front of me in a few different classes.

During my sophomore year in high school, there was another bully I had to contend with, who shall remain nameless. I had a locker that was within a foot or two of a classroom door. What coincidental bad luck. That same jerk of a bully attended class in that classroom. Many times I'd be at my locker switching out books when the school bell would go off, and out came that bully from the classroom. Just like Larry, he would always hassle me verbally. He was relentless. One day, as he was exiting the classroom, I was at my locker; I had a coat on. As he came out of the classroom, he grabbed a hold of the collar and yanked on it, and he said something to the effect, "Look at Ducky's coat." Well, that was the last straw. I had finally had enough. Full of anger, I faced him and slugged him a good one. He came back and hit me. The fight was on.

It must have lasted just a few minutes, and I came away with a black eye. I don't think I got in a good battle scar on him. After the fight, we went our separate ways. I was so fearful he was out for revenge, and for the next few days, I was 100% convinced he was going to try to beat me up again. I was on edge. Sure enough, by chance, we were walking toward one another in an empty hallway. I got really scared as I did not know what he might do. As we approached each other, I said to him, "Truce," and something to the effect I did not want to fight again. We passed each other, and nothing happened. What a sigh of relief. He never really bothered me again. More bullies are to come, so keep on reading.

Years later post-college and now working in the corporate world, I once again crossed paths with that bully. This time, it was in a bar that I had gone to after work on a Friday night to meet women. The bar had all the loud dance music and disco balls with colored lights swirling around the dance floor. I was checking out the women with a drink in my hand, when suddenly, from the opposite direction, I came face to face with the bully I had fought in high school. Now, that we were adults, I was no longer afraid of him. We said hello to each other and began a short conversation of small talk. I was dressed in a suit and tie. I looked dapper. The bully assumed I was now an attorney. (I must have had that attorney look down good because that was not the first-time strangers mistook me for an attorney.) I thought to myself, *YES! He thinks I must be a successful attorney.* I did confess what I actually did.

During that same sophomore year in high school, I came across my next opportunity to meet a girl. My father had a company privilege perk that came with his job, which was a country club membership for the use of entertaining clients. My father sold steel to manufacturers. In addition to entertaining clients, our family was allowed club privileges. I grew up swimming and playing golf there. Ironically, just my luck, Larry's family also had a membership at the country club. From what I could put together, Larry came from a well-to-do family. He never bothered me too much when we saw each other at the pool. We just avoided each other. Although, I think he was shocked the first time he saw me there as he didn't expect my family to be members. He never knew that we couldn't afford it. So that gave me some pleasure letting him believe we were affluent enough to be full-fledged members.

Because of the divorce, that summer Dad played the expected role of *weekend Dad.* He was an avid golfer and loved the game. We were always pursuing *his* interests; therefore, most of the time, we played golf. On one occasion while playing golf at the country club, there was a young girl playing alone behind us. She ended up having to wait for Dad and me to play. By this time, I recognized her. I will call her Penny. She was a fellow student from high school. She was an extremely attractive, conservative-looking girl, the next door type you would love to take home to meet Mom. She was exactly my type. However, I was out of her league. Instead of letting her play through, which is what I was hoping would happen, Dad asked her if she would like to join us. My first thought was, *Ah, hell No! Dad, don't do that!* This was embarrassing for me and extremely awkward. I was not that good at golf, and she was. I was nervous playing the rest of the course with her accompanying us. Well, we finally finished the round. Now, I could breathe a sigh of relief. Thank God that was over. Dad then suggested I ask her out and ask her to play the back nine. I took up my dad's recommendation.

A few days later after trying to build up the courage, I called her. Boy, I was so nervous. I started to dial the number on the old rotary phone. I only got a few numbers dialed when I chickened out and hung up. I tried a few times, again still being so nervous I couldn't go through with it. I'd dial the number, and right before it rang, I'd hang up. Boy, this was tough, stressful, and purely nerve-racking. Finally, I got up enough nerve to go through with it. I talked to her and asked her if she would like to play nine holes and have dinner afterward. She agreed. She said she'd be playing the front nine with her folks, and we'd play the back nine. So, we arranged a time that we would meet. I was psyched. This was going to be my first date ever! I was sixteen or seventeen at the time.

Mom lent me the car. I hand-washed that car so it looked spotlessly clean. I put on the best pair of pants I had at the time: grey corduroys. I arrived at the course with my golf clubs and waited at the end of the ninth hole for her to arrive with her family. Shortly, they arrived in a golf cart, but I noticed something was off. Her parents were in the front seats, and she was riding along back where the clubs were. But there was another girl with Penny. She looked to be the same age sitting next to her. Okay, something was up, and I started to get a bad feeling about this. Penny and her friend jumped off, and her parents drove off in the golf cart.

There I was, ready to go to play the back nine. She informed me that she didn't want to play because the friend who was with her was going to sleep over at her house. However, Penny suggested that the three of us walk over to the nearby putting green and have a friendly competition. *OH, BOY!* Suddenly, I became steamed with anger! But I had to keep my composure and not show I was annoyed. We putted for about twenty minutes. I was back home before dinner time. Very angry, I vented to Mom about what had happened. I was now 0-3.

In high school, I felt like I was hated by almost everyone. This, I think, was spurred on by all the teasing and bullying I suffered from when I was a little kid. I also perceived myself as an uncool nerd that nobody wanted to know. I had few friends. I was not a popular guy. I had one English class where there was three of the most beautiful cheerleaders. I so wanted to ask them all out but knew I would get turned down. They hung in a clique of snobby students, and I was not a star football player or Homecoming King. That was the level I would have to soar to if I was going to be able to have a shot at asking them out. Plus, in high school, I was still quite unsure of myself and had a confidence problem when it came to asking girls out. I flat out was too nervous.

Incidentally, with what I was going through with all my different issues, that's when I officially declared myself depressed while I sat at my desk one-afternoon doing homework. I was fifteen. That feeling of depression stayed with me until I reached age 60.

My junior year of high school was average, and I was still being hassled by the usual suspects. However, there was an incident that took place in the gym locker room after class. For my birthday, I received a cool new shirt, and I was wearing it for the first time. As we were changing back into our street clothes, I had just put my jeans on and was shirtless. I had turned around for a second, perhaps to throw something in the trash, but as I turned back around toward the locker, my shirt was *GONE!* I must have had my back turned for no more than three seconds.

I became emotionally upset internally as this was just another assailant picking on me.

I loved that shirt. I looked all around in the trash cans and asked the others in the locker room if they had seen who took my shirt; of course, nobody saw anything. I found myself in another jam. I had no shirt to wear. As a last resort, I threw on my smelly gym shirt; I knew I could not go to class like this. I skipped my next class, called my mom, and had her bring me another shirt to wear. It was times like these while in high school I felt like everyone was out to get me. I only had around three friends at the time.

During that same year, I developed a crush on another girl. I will call her Karen. She sat next to me in biology class. She was the first girl I ever wanted to marry. I am a hopeless romantic, and I thought how romantic it would be later in life if I could claim, "I married my high school sweetheart." She was always well put together with beautiful short brown hair and a nice all-around personality. It's no wonder she became my next crush. I had noticed that she was volunteering in the library, so I would sometimes hang out there. Now, I had to get up the nerve to ask her out. This was no easy task, looking back on my past rejections.

I finally gathered up the courage after developing my plan. I had also noticed that on some days, she would be at a study carrel. On the day I picked to ask her out at the study carrel, I was mentally prepared and focused. I approached the study carrel from the opposite side. She saw me sit down opposite her, as that was part of my plan. Within a few minutes, I tossed a handwritten note up and over the common divider. Yes, it was still a juvenile way of asking her out. It brought back flashbacks of the girl in junior high. I did not have the nerve to ask her out directly. Heck, it was all I could do to muster up the courage to toss her the note. This time, the note was more of an adult nature and asked if she'd be interested in going out Saturday night. I was too excited about her response that I didn't wait for her to toss it back to me with an answer. I stood up and then asked her out. I think Karen was caught off guard as could be expected by a note flying out of the blue. Her response to me was, "Well, I'm going to have to ask my mom." *Well, okay,* I thought. *A bit odd, but okay.*

The next time I saw her was in biology class. We sat down awkwardly at the same table. I'm now dying for an answer. Then she spoke up in an awkward and reluctant way and told me that her grandma was having surgery, so she would have to stay home. 0-4.

Another time in the same class, an awkward situation happened. Our teacher handed out a four-page assignment. It was science-related yet involved an algebraic nature. I think it had something to do with multiplying genes. Math is my worst subject, and I'm not good with algebra. I was not able to understand or complete the assignment. I seemed to be the only one in class who did not understand it. The teacher asked for volunteers for someone to tutor me. Nobody raised his/her hand. That just added to the poor self-image I had of myself of why I was unpopular. To my surprise, Karen suddenly raised her hand. *Wow! I can't believe she is willing to help after rejecting me.* We agreed to meet for an hour of tutoring. At the end of the session, I still couldn't comprehend it. She was nice enough to let me keep her assignment. I had gone on to ask her out a few more times and kept getting shot down. However, I still have her copy of that assignment to this day, and it remains in pristine condition.

As I entered my senior year of high school, it was on the first or second day when I was walking down one of the hallways of the school. On my right, I saw a group of girls congregating around a girl's locker. There were probably four of them. As I walked past them, one of the girls casually singled me out to her friends and subtly pointed at me. The girl who did it I knew by name but didn't actually know her. I wasn't quite sure what to make of it. But I interpreted it as a positive that she was pointing to her friends that she liked me.

I will call this girl Maxine. She became my love interest for my senior year. Mind you, I am not putting all my eggs in one basket. There were others who caught my eye but none that captured my attention like Maxine did. While driving to school and parking in the student lot, I got a chance to see what car she drove. One day when I was finished with all my classes, I was heading to my car in the student lot to head home. Coincidentally, so was Maxine. Because I was smitten with her, so out of curiosity, I decided to follow her to see where she lived. I was not stalking her. There's a difference. I was infatuated with her romantically. It's only natural that I wanted to learn all about her. That was my intent, not for evil purposes. So, as I followed her home, it turned out she lived in the neighborhood adjacent to mine. It was a step up into a wealthier neighborhood than where I lived. So, I drove on by, and it was cool in a romantic, interesting way to see what kind of home she lived in.

The school year wore on. It was now the second and last semester of school, and I signed up for a typing class. I knew I'd need typing for college-level term papers and for the future. On the first day of class, I sat down at a desk with a typewriter on it. I noticed Maxine was in my class, and she selected the desk behind me, off to my left. I was elated. Now, maybe I would have some opportunity to have a conversation to get to know her rather than those juvenile love notes. Still at my age of nineteen, I was still very green on how to approach women. I was still not able to find a courageous way to talk to her during that semester. Still intimidated and shy around girls, I couldn't muster up anything to talk to her about without feeling stupid. (Actually, I prefer it if a girl makes the first move or gives me some clear indication that they like me. This comes from years of being rejected and turned down when asking for a first date. That way, I know they like me; therefore, I don't have to worry necessarily about being rejected.)

Over the course of the semester, she made no effort to show that she liked me. So, here's what I tried to do. Every time the typing teacher was lecturing and we were not typing, I would turn sideways in my chair and lean my back against the wall. And I would look at her, not constantly, but a noteworthy number of times. I hope I didn't give off a creepy vibe. It was totally innocent on my part if it came across that way. I *desperately* wanted her to *notice* me. Guess you could say I was trying to establish eye contact (that's what I've always heard is to try to establish eye contact). Only occasionally would she give me a glance. When I would turn around, on a very rare occasion, she would look over at me and give me half a smile. That enhanced my ego. *YES! Positive progress! Maybe she really does like me*, I thought. But the opportunity never arose for a shy guy like me to ask her out. Looking back on it now, I must have put her in an uncomfortable situation. I know it would make me feel awkward if I were in her shoes, unless, of course, I liked the person looking at me.

When the yearbook came out, I asked her to sign mine. I was hoping for something romantic, indicating she wanted to date me. She wrote something short, lame, and corny with no indication of wanting to date me. That was a big letdown. I guess the gesture I saw her make toward me at the beginning of the school year was not what I thought it was. Perhaps, she was pointing me out as a nerd, or I was the butt of a joke.

After I graduated from high school, I did not give up. She was a junior in high school at the time. It was now summer. I found her family's phone number in the phone book. I called her. However, it was not that easy. I was nervous as hell and shaking in my shoes. It took me several attempts before I'd actually hear the phone ringing on her end. I'd keep hanging up as I dialed, or once I dialed, I'd hang up before it rang. It was extremely difficult for me to ask someone out. It wasn't so much fear of rejection, but it was the fear of what if they said yes. You see in my mind, if they said yes, then it would bring a whole new level of pressure. *What would I plan for the date?* I worried. *What if I'd screw up?* That's the biggest fear I had back in those days. When I finally had the nerve to ride it out with all the bravery I could muster, I let it ring. To my amazement, she said yes! *AWESOME!* Finally, my first real date!

After hanging up the phone, I realized I had a major problem on my hands. Since I knew where she lived, it didn't occur to me, in all my nervousness, to ask her where she lived. If I just showed up, it would look creepy. So, now I had myself a dilemma. I realized I had to call her back and ask for her address. I let a day or two go by before calling her back for her address and playing dumb. I suddenly detected a negative hesitation in her voice. Something was not right. She took an awkward pause. It occurred to me then that she did not want to go out. And I sure as hell didn't want to go out with her if it would be an awkward date where neither of us wanted to be with the other. I wasn't going to waste my time that way. So, before she could turn me down, I asked her if she still wanted to go out. Again, there was a long pause, so I replied, "Am I putting you on the spot?" She immediately said, "Yes, you are putting me on the spot." Well, that was that. We never went out. 0-5. Crash and burn into the wall. I struck out again.

I was never able to get a date in my entire four years of high school. Can you imagine what that did for my confidence with women? I was interested in plenty of girls. But the opportunity wasn't right to ask someone out, or I just got too nervous. It's embarrassing to admit that I could not even get *one* date in high school. It was just the luck of the draw I was delt. You may be wondering why I have gone into such detail about my unlucky love life. I'm mentioning it because I'm taking you on my journey that's leading up to something that *may* surprise you later in the book.

Fast forward to my thirties. Having now graduated from college and working in the corporate world, I was still single, never married, and unlucky in love for all the years that had since passed. By this time in my life, all my friends seemed to have found the right ingredients to find someone to marry. I was still trying to figure out what those magic ingredients were.

The story with Maxine did not end that summer after graduating high school. It was circa 1990s. I found myself on Friday nights gravitating to bars (and doing a little bar hopping) and looking for a female that would capture my fancy. I never went to dive bars. I frequented bars that had a professional clientele.

As I was strolling through the bar, drink in hand and dressed in a suit and tie as I had just come from work, I was waiting to see which attractive woman caught my eye to approach. As I was walking, I saw a very attractive woman sitting at a table with another female. I walked up to the woman who had caught my attention with the intent of asking her out. She suddenly told me to come with her. So, I followed her around to the front door lobby area, wondering what was going on as she seemed to be acting a bit weird. Once we reached the lobby, she stated, "I'm Maxine." Now, I suddenly *recognized* her twenty years later! She gave me her phone number, and suddenly I'm thinking, *after all these years later, I have a second chance with her!* (What I didn't understand was why she would drag me all the way to the front of the bar to tell me this. Did I embarrass her just by being me? Or was she ashamed to talk to me in front of her friend because I was not good enough for her to carry on a conversation in front of her friend? It was very strange behavior.)

I let some days go by and then called her to see if she would like to meet for a drink at a place I knew. She said she had plans but could meet the following night. Okay, fine, that sounded legitimate. So, prior to meeting her, I started to reminisce in my head and figured we were both more mature in our thirties, and I had certainly come a long way and was not that afraid to talk to women. Now, finally she was interested.

We got our drinks. *We can catch up on what we've both been doing since high school.* We talked briefly for about twenty minutes or less. Then, out of the blue, she suddenly announced that the plans she claimed the night before were for tonight and that she had screwed up and needed to leave. *EXPLETIVE! EXPLETIVE!* I said to myself. *It is obvious now that she never liked me.* This was another rejection to shamefully hang on the metaphoric wall.

Chapter 11

Stonehenge

One of the highlights of my life started in high school. Before I get into the meat of this chapter, I would like to preface it with some retrospective insight. Twenty/twenty hindsight tells me I should have pursued a career in some form within the music industry. More accurately, I should have gone to a trade school that could teach the mechanics of how to work a mixing console in a recording studio or something behind the scenes in music. I love being around musicians and live music. I have the greatest respect for musicians and deep envy because they can do something I cannot. I so wish I had their talent. From a very young age, I have had a love for music. I like many different genres of music, classic rock being my favorite.

When I was in grade school, my mom forced me, and I say forced because I did not want to take piano lessons. I hated practicing. I took lessons from Jack's mother. I felt at the time that it was a bit effeminate for a young boy to play piano. Mind you, circa 1967, there were no solo male role models who were rock and roll piano players around at the time. After two years, I quit. I harbor huge regrets now that I'm older. I wish I could play and write my own songs. It was not until I got into junior high school that Elton John appeared on the scene. Then, years later, Billy Joel came along. Had these two wonderful piano players been around, I would not have quit.

In junior high, I still remembered enough piano to get by to write my first six finished/unfinished songs. They were extremely elementary-level songs written mainly with only the right hand in mind. I still have them to this day in mint condition. This was my own personal dip into the water of wanting to be a singer/songwriter.

Back in my freshman year of high school, I was introduced to my current, one and only, music writing partner, Charles Brown. We were introduced through a mutual friend. Charles and I had known of each other going back to the eighth grade, but we were just students who saw each other around school, nothing more. Once we were formally introduced, I found out that he was in a band called Terraplane.

After having officially met Charles and discovered that he played guitar in a rock band, a light bulb went off in my mind. I jumped at the chance to try to form a new band with Charles. He was receptive to the idea. So, I was able to get Charles to leave Terraplane and start our own band. At that point in time, my favorite band was the Beatles. I knew that they wrote their own songs, and if we were to be successful, I told Charles we would need to write our own music as well. I had no interest in being a cover band playing "Hits." Since I could not play an instrument but felt I'd be good with lyrics, I pitched my idea to Charles: "Why don't I write the lyrics, and you write the music? We'd be a Bernie Taupin/Elton John style writing team."

Starting out of the gate in the beginning, my written lyrics left something to be desired. However, Charles did a pretty good job applying music to them. As the years progressed, I've become much better at writing lyrics, having studied lyric writing by various artists along with their form and style. Charles has also come a long way since I first met him. He has become much better at writing music; in fact, he has reached the level of a professional session player in my opinion. Charles has mentioned to me in recent years that he hates writing lyrics because it feels like an English assignment. As for me, I can really get "in the zone" writing lyrics. I love writing poetry as well. So, we are the perfect fit. In fact, we respect each other's job so much that to make our songs work, if there becomes a problem, such as a line or a stanza that's not working with his melody, we make suggestions to each other where we need to rework the lyrics to make the song the best it can be. Charles may give me a suggestion on where I need to correct the issue, then run the reworked lyrics by Charles for his opinion. He will say, "You're the lyric guy," trusting I will make a proper correction. A response, in kind, may come from me if I feel something should be changed musically or give him direction based upon the lyrics/topic I had in mind when I wrote the lyrics.

Charles and I were starting to become great friends in high school, having met in 1974. He then turned me on to The Who. Silly me, I had never even heard of The Who. I had heard of The Guess Who but not The Who. Well, I became drunk in love with the music of The Who, so much so that I became a *Who-a-holic*. I loved my quest of discovering the complete catalog of what The Who had put out at that time circa 1964-1977. I am forever grateful to Charles for introducing me to their music. Within a few months and over the next few years, I had purchased The Who's entire catalog, including all the solo works by each member of the band, as well. From 1974 to the present day, they have been my all-time favorite band. Starting in 1976, I have seen them, including solo shows by two members of the band Roger Daltrey and John Entwistle, thirty-five times over my life span. We had all the intentions of becoming the next The Who.

From the birth of our band in 1974 to the present day, I have written 128 lyrical songs, and I continue writing lyrics when an idea hits me. In addition, I have countless other unfinished lyrics, stanzas, and cleverly written lines waiting to be used. Charles has not put music to all of them but has some riffs for certain songs that are not musically completed. In our junior year of high school, Charles gave me some devastating news. He informed me that his dad was getting transferred with his job and that they were relocating to Houston, Texas. That threw a major monkey wrench into our hopeful rock 'n' roll future plans. However, we were still determined to remain a songwriting team.

Long before our junior year of high school, we had lined up a drummer and a bass player, all from the same high school. But as a full band, it was not to be. We had never even practiced together. I was taking the position of lead singer, pattering ourselves after The Who. It was only a makeshift band at best. We were just building the foundation of the roots of the band that never came to fruition. We had gone through countless band names, always trying to improve the name over the last one. We must have changed the name at least five times. I think I was the one always changing it because I didn't like what we came up with. One that I remember I loved at the time sounds so stupid today. It was Flying High. *Really?* How awful it was and uncool sounding now. Charles and

I are fascinated with the United Kingdom. So, I got *serious* and wanted to have a name that reflected something British. My folks had a book on the United Kingdom that had some great pictures. I went through that book, flipping page by page, looking for a cool-sounding name. I came across a photo of Stonehenge. Bingo! That was it! The perfect name is STONEHENGE. We refer to Stonehenge to this day if we are talking about one of our songs. When I lyrically write a new song, I will send it to Charles via email, and in the subject line, I write, "Stonehenge Song," followed by the title.

We both fell in love with the name Stonehenge to the point that Charles created our Stonehenge logo, which inspired me to design our Stonehenge coat of arms. To design the coat of arms, I drew a design I saw on my mother's cigarette package of *Pall Mall Golds*. It had a coat of arms that I used as a guide to tailor the design to fit what Stonehenge was all about. Charles's logo design consisted of a few stone pillars with a huge bursting sun shining widely behind the pillars. It was fabulous! I added the word Stonehenge below in an old English font. Now, we had logos like that of The Rolling Stones, the lips and tongue, and The Who's target. We were so motivated at the time with our newfound band; we *were* going to make it big one day in the vision of our naïve, inexperienced minds.

In the summer of 1975 between our ninth and tenth-grade summer, The Who's rock opera film *Tommy* was released. It was playing at a large theater. (Back in those days, there weren't many multi-theater plexuses, and large theaters were still the norm.) *Tommy* was only being shown at one theater in Denver, the Aladdin. It was old and had a middle eastern motif. For the first time ever, there was this rock 'n' roll type sound system. I have never seen this set up like this before or since. *Tommy* was billed as a film where "Your Senses Will Never Be The Same." And they sure weren't after seeing this movie! The theater had installed huge speakers in all four corners of the theater. The speakers had to be at least four feet tall and at least three and a half feet wide. I had never seen anything like it. Man, it was LOUD! And very pleasing to the rock 'n' roll ear. Note: IF IT'S TOO LOUD, THEN YOU'RE TOO OLD. We were both blown away and creatively influenced by the film.

Stonehenge Coat of Arms

Stonehenge logo

As a result I got inspired to write a rock opera myself and have Charles set the music to it. It was called *Marco*. The premise was that Marco came from across the universe as a messiah and saved everyone from what I don't know. I never got beyond the first five songs. It was very elementary. For The Who fans out there, it was comparable to "A Quick One While He's Away."

Then roughly a year later, I wrote a full-fledged, seventeen-song rock opera with some instrumental songs thrown in entitled *Phantasmagoria*. The story is about a high school-age kid who doesn't get along with his parents and is frustrated with life. He decides to run away and falls asleep in a field. As he falls asleep for the night, his mind starts to drift off into an abstract dream of this fantasy world where he becomes a messiah for all people. He became extremely famous worldwide. His followers turn against him. He falls from grace and becomes hated by everyone. Then he wakes up and realizes it was all a dream. The final song of the rock opera, "I'd Sing Out to Feel Sorry", raps up his fictional life as a lost soul. I took parts of my own life and frustration and wrote them into the rock opera. Years later, it dawned on me it pretty much followed the storyline of *Tommy*. However, at the time I wrote it, I thought I was being totally original. Incidentally, Charles sent the song "I'd Sing Out to Feel Sorry" into a songwriting contest, as we both thought it was one of our best songs, hoping we might win. On the contrary, our song got reviewed and rejected mainly because we did not have a hook. We were both disappointed.

Then in 2021, we submitted another song to a writing contest. A true story of the acquaintance we crossed paths with called "The Man I'd Never Get to Know". Charles and I lost this competition also. Oh well, 0-2. What can you do? We tried.

After Charles moved away during our junior year in high school, we continued to write together. I always continued to forward my lyrics to Charles. Over the years, he has found time to put music to some of them and the others sit on the shelf. I tend to write in a rock 'n' roll manner that is similar to The Who. Charles has informed me that every song I send him he will make it sound as hard rock as The Who's "The Real Me" unless I instruct him otherwise. Some of the lyrics I pull from real-life experiences and others may be a ballad of pure fiction.

Once I graduated from high school, my communication with Charles began to drift. In my freshman year in college, 1978-1979, I wrote a series of new lyrics and sent them to him as if it were for a new album entitled Hard Tracks. I designed an album cover for it.

Charles and I lost touch after that for many years. Since I enjoyed writing, and I had no one to write music with anymore, that's when I turned to writing poetry.

After close to seventeen years, just by pure chance—dumb luck—I happened to be in a record store in Denver, Colorado, when lo and behold in walks Charles. I went up to him and said hello, and our friendship picked up again; Stonehenge was back up and running.

The collaboration I'm most proud of is "The Man I'd Never Get to Know". It's a ballad about a real gentleman, whom we both met who had a lot of promise in the business world for a professional career, and suddenly his young life was taken without warning. We were both devastated hearing the sad news. It prompted me to honor him with a poem that morphed into a song honoring his life. The following is the backstory as to how the song came about.

Charles and I were staying at the Las Vegas Hard Rock Hotel. We had flown in to see The Who in concert. Inside the hotel was a high-end men's clothing store called "John Varvatos." In the back of the store, they sold classic rock and roll records. Being two rock and roll guys, we were lured to the back to evaluate what they had. We were then approached by an impeccably dressed young man in a suit. His name was Danny. He was very well-spoken and asked if he could be of assistance. We politely answered, "No, we're only here to check out your record collection." We pulled out a few classics, *Tommy*, by The Who and the Woodstock albums and explained to him the importance they had in the history of rock 'n' roll. Danny became instantly intrigued by our knowledge and replied, "See, I need to know this stuff." After all, the hotel was mostly filled with classic rock memorabilia mounted to walls throughout the hotel as like a Hard Rock Cafe. A genre long since passed by the time Danny was born, he was unfamiliar with the items throughout the hotel. We were impressed by him because he was very mature and didn't seem like your typical young person. He had an aura about him that I just *knew* he was going to succeed at climbing the corporate ladder. Over the course of our four-day stay, we would run into him several more times and expand his knowledge about classic rock and point out that John Entwistle, bassist for The Who, died in that hotel from a cocaine overdose in 2002.

Less than five months later, either Roger Daltrey or The Who were back in Vegas, and again, we stayed at the same hotel. We were excited to see Danny again and educate him more since he sparked a yearning desire to learn. After checking in and settling in our rooms, we went back to the "John Varvatos" store and asked for him. We were informed that he was hit and killed by a car. My stomach dropped. I was shaken. I teared up. I told the guy how impressed we were with Danny, and I immediately said aloud that I was going to write a poem to honor him. I asked the employee if he knew Danny's last name because I'd like to share whatever I wrote with his family. He complied. We left the store, and Charles asked if he could put music to it as he knew Danny, as well. Now, that would mean I would have to come up with a chorus, which I did. This is the longest lyrical song I've ever written. This could *not* be a rock song. In order to get the somber mood across in the melody to obtain how I envisioned my lyrics to reflect, I told Charles to use "Daniel" by Elton John and "Leon" from Roger Daltrey's solo album *One of The Boys* as a guide. In the song, I made references to The Who. For non-Who fans, the references I made are "The Ox," a nickname John Entwistle had, and I use the word "moon" to refer to The Who's drummer, Keith Moon.

I've listed the URL and lyrics to "The Man I'd Never Get to Know". If you care to hear the recorded version directly, use this URL to hear the song. https://soundcloud.com/user-972729743/the-man-id-never-get-to-know

William Cowell Duckworth

The Man I'd Never Get to Know

Came across a chance encounter with a man I'd never get to know.
And Danny, you weren't just the average Joe.
I could see there was something different about you.
Danny, you made a positive impression on me.

You were young and missed the classic era of golden rock 'n' roll.
Surrounded by a gold mine of rock glory you didn't understand.

Danny....oh Danny,
You left us much too soon.
You never got to hear the stories of the MOON.
You missed the magic and pleasure of classic rock and roll.
Now I'm gonna miss your soul.

We met by chance and the conversation quickly turned to rock and roll.
Suddenly I had your attention and your thirst for knowledge.
So, unlike the peers of your generation.
I began to open your doors for comprehension.

We met again during your break.
I explained to you the OX.
Who died above you from, from the school of hard knocks.

Danny....oh Danny,
You left us much too soon.
You never got to hear the stories of the MOON.
You missed the magic and pleasure of classic rock and roll.
Now I'm gonna miss your soul.

Prior to leaving for home, we exchanged cards.
Allowing me to further your rock knowledge.
Once home I knew just what to do.
Send you video on the history of THE WHO.

Now less than a year has passed.
I returned as my plane touched down again.
Back in town for another rock event.
You were on my mind to educate you more.

Beaming with excitement to say HELLO.
Was sadly informed you had lost your life.
For me it was a shock and hard to take.
But I cared enough to write this for your sake.

You carried yourself so well.
You were set apart from all the rest.
Just knew you were headed for a promising destiny.
But without warning your candle burned out.

Danny....oh Danny,
You left us much too soon.
You never got to hear the stories of the MOON.
You missed the magic and the pleasure of classic rock and roll.
Now I'm gonna miss your soul.

Lyrics by BILL DUCKWORTH and Music by CHARLES BROWN

I have never worked on a song as hard as this one. Once home, I sat down and organized all my written ideas and arranged them into stanzas and created a chorus. It took me four hours straight to put the lyrics together. The journey from writing this song to contacting his family had been a labor of love. Many years went by, and after a hard search, I was able to locate his mother in October of 2022. We sent her the written back story of our encounter with her son, the written lyrics, and a copy of the song on CD. Unfortunately, we never heard back.

Chapter 12

The College Years

I was finally glad I graduated high school and was done with it. I was free from all the bullies that I'd never have to deal with again. I never viewed graduating high school as a major milestone in my life. It was no different to me than moving on from junior high school.

School had always been extremely hard for me due to my learning disabilities. I have dyslexia and am an extremely slow reader. I am unable to memorize, which hindered me while taking tests. In addition, I also suffer from convergence inefficiency. As a result, I graduated from high school with around a 2.0 GPA. This obviously excluded me from attending great colleges. So, upon graduation, my initial plan was to attend junior college in Kansas City, where my dad and his wife lived, and I would live in their basement. Dad had married his new wife when I was in high school back in Denver. I had hoped to build that long-desired strong bond that I had never had with him. I had always sought my mom's and dad's approval, but I never got it, which, in turn, added to the ingredients of having a poor self-image.

After graduating from high school and entering the summer months, my relationship with my dad was not getting any better. Mom and my psychiatrist at the time who was a good friend of the family, *strongly* advised me not to make the move to Kansas City, as they pointed out, and rightly so, things probably would not go well with Dad and me. They were correct. So, that summer I applied to a four-year college in western Colorado.

College was a real struggle for me to earn that degree. I attended three colleges. There were bleak times when some of the needed requirements to graduate were so difficult on more than one occasion that I thought I might never graduate. That bachelor's degree I earned means a lot to me, and it can never be taken away.

When I entered my thirties, I realized that having a college degree didn't really put me that far ahead. As I enter my golden years, knowing what I know now, I took the wrong path. How was I to know that at nineteen? I wish I could go back and get a second shot at it.

I found the first college I attended to be a joke. In my opinion, it *SUCKED!* I hated every minute I was there between 1978 and 1980. The campus wasn't much bigger than my high school. My high school was large and spread out as a mini-college campus. I had a very bad experience my freshman year while living in the dorms. It was a complete disaster.

My dorm experience was the worst part that a particular college had to offer. The interior was very cheap in appearance. My side of the building housed approximately fifteen male students. We were provided with a small community bathroom, which consisted of two urinals, two toilet stalls, three sinks, and two small showers. It was not ideal when everyone was trying to get ready in the morning at the same time for class. It got worse. The room I was assigned was aesthetically cold and uninviting to the eye.

My dorm room was one step up in comfort from that of an actual prison cell. The college went to *no* expense to make freshman students welcome, knowing they'd be living here for the school year. There was nothing cozy about it. It had a white, industrial-tiled floor like you would find in a medical office. There was cheap furniture bolted to the wall, made out of inexpensive wood, and a cheap slab of plastic to use as a desktop, tiny closet space, cheap bookshelves, and, to top it off, a Murphy bed made out of what appeared to be a three-inch slab of wood and four-inch-thick mattress. The whole lot was bolted to the wall and looked like a self-assembly kit for $300 found on a television infomercial that you could assemble in an afternoon, complete with screws, washers, and bolts. There was no need for a hammer. Oh yeah, this college *really* rolled out the welcome mat. The only thing lacking was a welcome sign on the wall that read, "We hope you enjoy your stay with us." I've seen cheap hotel rooms that were more inviting than that crap. When my classes were over and on the weekends, I would have to live in my near prison-style accommodation.

I was assigned a roommate who turned out to be a first-class jerk! We had nothing in common and did not get along. He was one of the most inconsiderate people I have ever met. At one point, over a dispute about rooming together, he threatened to beat me up. It was at that point that I moved out and was able to get another room to myself.

While having the new dorm room to myself was almost heaven, it was to be short-lived. I was told I'd be getting a new roommate. He was a freaky-looking weirdo student with a homeless appearance. He was transitioning from a halfway house. I had seen him around campus. When I came home from classes one day, in my dorm room sat this campus weirdo. *Oh, please tell me this ain't so,* I thought. He was also bullied by the students on the floor so badly that once he was so freaked out, he cried.

We were not a good fit either. The breaking point came when I entered the room one night; there were about five to six people sitting around smoking pot. Now, I had the concern that if he was caught in the room smoking pot, he could get busted, and I might get busted with him. That was it! No more dorm living for me! I moved out and moved into a home with a private entrance, bathroom, and bedroom. It came with *real* furniture. This was the Hilton compared to dorm living!

I had no dates during my freshman year of college. I did find one girl I liked, but my shyness in how to approach her got the better of me, and I missed the opportunity. I'm sure fear of rejection added to it as well.

Second Year of College/Flunking Out

My second year of college is when I cut loose, fell into the party scene, and had my first date *EVER* at age twenty! My new digs for college this year were living in the basement of another house with two roommates. We all had separate bedrooms and shared a bathroom. Up to this point in life, I had never drunk alcohol, not even a beer. Oh, I had tasted beer in the past, but I didn't like it.

I was still the shy innocent kid up to this point. One of my new roommates knew I did not like the taste of alcohol. So, one night we went to the local college bar that had a dance floor and a DJ who played music—all the popular songs. Disco had just hit the music scene around two years earlier. Upon arrival, my roommate recommended I try a German beer with a smooth taste. I ordered one and yes, sir, I certainly did like it. It became my beverage of choice in the coming months. This was my baptism into the college life of partying. I soon became a regular at that bar. I'd be there every FAC (Friday Afternoon Club) and on ladies' and Saturday nights, as well.

As the school year wore on, my grades began to suffer. I began to notice this young lady was always at the college bar, too. She caught my attention. We must have exchanged eye contact many times. Again, I'm shy and never asked her to dance as I couldn't dance. My roommate was kind enough to teach me a few steps and how to move to the music. A few weeks later after having got up the nerve to ask this girl to dance, which was not easy, I was scared to death. The reason was I didn't know what to say to girls or how to act. I was too worried I'd screw up in front of them, and they wouldn't want to be seen with me.

I finally got up the nerve to dance with her. I still remember what the song was, "Don't Stop Till You Get Enough" by Michael Jackson. To this day, when I hear that song, I think of her. I still love that song. I danced with her every time the DJ played that song. I finally got the nerve to ask her out. She said Yes! I was excited but didn't put much stock in it since my past luck with girls was not successful.

Well, things were going to plan. I went to pick her up and found she lived in a trailer. We actually got in my car and drove off to see the movie *Time After Time*. TOUCHDOWN! and I spiked the ball! I finally had my first date, and she didn't cancel! Now, I'm 1-5. She told me she was twenty and divorced and was not a college student but worked at a rental car agency at the local airport. According to her, she got married to her high school boyfriend to escape living with her mom. The marriage was short-lived.

I find humor in the fact that my first date was with a *divorcee* at the age of twenty-one. I was on cloud nine. I fell hard and fast for this woman. I wanted to marry her and live happily ever after. How naive could I have been? It turns out that I later found she was promiscuous just by watching her over the school year with different guys, and it became clear. Things between us did not last long. However, before things went south, she once invited me over to watch *Saturday Night Live* (*SNL*). She had to work till around 10 p.m. and *SNL* came on at 10:30 p.m. I was so dumb and green back then, dating the first girl who ever went out with me. I thought I was just going over to watch *SNL* and leave afterward. Well, as the show progressed, she was sitting next to me, and I wanted to make a move, but again, I was too shy. *WAKE UP, BILL! IT'S SO OBVIOUS SHE WANTS YOU TO MAKE A MOVE!* She then grabbed my hand. I liked that, but not having any other experience with women, I missed the cue of what to do next. A little more time went by as the show continued, and out of the blue, she kissed me on my cheek. *NOW,* I'm picking up on the romantic signs. *Finally, Bill! Welcome to the party!* We then started to make out lips-to-lips only. That's how I thought you kissed. I did not even know what French kissing was. I had heard of the term but not the definition. We then both lay down on the sofa. I laid on top of her, and we spent the remainder of the night fully clothed, kissing lips to lips. I eventually fell asleep on top of her. Only months later did it occur to me that I could have slept with her. I wouldn't have anyway because back at that time, I did not believe in sex till marriage. She ended up dumping me, but I kept trying to pursue her. That summer, she took the time to write a *Dear John* letter to me that was about ten pages long and why she couldn't carry on a relationship. I respected that. It gave me closure and explained why she wanted to dump me. I hold no ill will toward her.

The partying continued. One of my roommates often smoked pot. He asked me if I wanted to smoke it with him, but I was too strait-laced back then. I did, however, remember when I was in high school, Mom had told me she smoked it twice, once with a cousin and then with some of her girlfriends. Of course, I was shocked as this did not seem like something she would do. So, during that second year of college, I happened to be home for one of the holidays, and I told Mom that my roommate invited me to try it. She responded with, "You should at least try it once." Whoa, she approved. However, I still felt it was wrong.

Back at college, I had a change of heart. After classes one afternoon, I was ready to go for it. I knocked on my roommate's door and said, "I'm ready to try the pot." He seemed to be having some excitement in his demeanor and did not hesitate to produce his stash. He pulled out a little pot pipe that was only two to three inches long. He inserted a little hard, compressed rock-like piece of marijuana into the pipe. I had never seen marijuana in that form before. Years later, I came to believe it may have been hash. I took a few deep hits off it and held the smoke in so it could get into my system. I was expecting instant results (as that's how I always thought marijuana affected you), and I felt nothing. I told my roommate, and he probably said something like, "Just wait." Sure enough, after about five minutes, it hit me like a freight train. Immediately, I was high as a kite. My roommate took a few hits, too. We then went to a store where he needed some items for class. While at the store, I was really spacing out. I just stood still, staring at a stand-up rack of items that rotated in a circle. I was having a hard time concentrating. One second, I'd be in reality, and the next second, I'd be in an altered state. I became paranoid as a result of smoking the pot because I was just staring the whole time at the stand-up rack and afraid someone would call the cops since I was not moving. I was kind of in a trance, trying to make sense out of what I was going through.

Once back at the house, I tried to sleep it off, but it wasn't working. By the time early evening came, I walked over to the student center to eat dinner. After dinner, I went home and hung out some more. I was not in shape for studying as the pot high was slowly starting to wear off. The next thing I knew, Mom called to check-in. That was a tough phone call to pay attention to while still being somewhat high. Later that year, I told Mom I was high during that call, and she could tell something was off with me. Anyway, after about five hours, I had come back to full reality and was totally sober. That experience scared me at the time.

Later during the school year, while hanging out with the party crowd, I was offered pot as they passed it around. Under peer pressure, I took the joint and *FAKED* inhaling, as I was still afraid of pot at that time due to my initial experience. And no, I'm not using Bill Clinton's excuse, "I did not inhale." I put it up to my closed lips and waited a second or two to give the appearance I inhaled, then I passed the joint on to the next guy.

As the school year progressed, I started getting more confidence with women and asked more of them out. I had some regular, normal dates but ran back into the bad luck times I experienced in high school. Three such instances where one girl agreed to go out and then canceled on me. Now, came the *first,* but not last time, I got stood up. I asked a girl out that I thought was interested in me, having briefly talked to her a few times. On the day of the date, I washed the car, showered, and got all ready for the night out. That night, I drove to her house and saw her car outside. It was dark out, and not one light was on at the house. Strange. I began to get a bad feeling about this. I went to the door and rang the bell. There was no answer, no sound of movement inside the house. I rang the bell again. Then, after a bit of delay, I knocked on the door. *NOTHING!* Now, I determined I was stood up. I was steaming mad and probably said a few choice words. I must have stood on her porch for at least five minutes before giving up. I returned home. My roommate was surprised I returned so early. I explained to him what happened while still in an angry mood. He told me I must confront her the next time I saw her and ask her what the deal was with her standing me up. The next day, I caught her at dinner at the cafeteria in the Student Center. Oh boy, I had to confront her now. This was going to be very awkward, and I wished I could skip this uncomfortable situation. But it had to be done, and I could not let her get away with standing me up! I confronted her, and she replied, "I was there," She replied. She was playing stupid. I assumed that at the last minute, she chickened out and went out partying with her friends. I was never interested in asking her out again.

The last unfortunate date I had at college that year was a gal who used me. This would not be the first or last time I got used. It's happened many times since. Anyway, there was this attractive girl I asked out that I had talked to on campus a few times. She had agreed to go out with me. I did the usual preparation for the date, washed the car, and dressed up. This gal seemed to be a bit classier than the other girls I dated. So, I asked her to dinner at a high-class place, and then we would go downstairs afterward to the bar, where they had dancing to a DJ and colored spotlights swirling around the dance floor.

The high-class establishment had white tablecloths and elegant place settings. I noticed that they had lobster and wine on the menu. When the waiter came, we gave our order. Wouldn't you know it? She ordered the lobster and a bottle of wine, which came to the table in a silver stand in a bucket of ice that stood next to the table. I could see what was happening here. She ordered the most expensive thing on the menu. Obviously, she was taking full advantage of me. I probably had a steak. Once we finished dinner, we went downstairs to dance in the bar. I could sense the whole night there was no connection between us. We didn't stay long. When I took her back to her dorm, I was sure hoping she'd invite me in. Now, I was not looking to sleep with her. I was just hoping for a good chat where we could get to know each other, and after a bit, I'd be on my way. As I turned into her dorm parking lot, I could tell by something she said that she was ending the date, and I had no chance of coming up. I never asked her out again, either.

Well, finals for the end of the school year were approaching. I had spent most of the school year heavily falling into the party scene. I developed a bunch of new party friends that I got together with nearly every night. In that college town, you could find a raging party on a Monday night, not to mention the rest of the week. I now realized there was a good chance I would be flunking out. I often would not go to class for whatever reason, and I'm sure hangovers were part of it. It was funny; I would meet up with my partying group of classmates at breakfast with a hangover, not in the mood to party that night. Someone would mention there was a party that night somewhere, and I was not feeling it at breakfast time. Come lunch I would be feeling a bit better and would start to consider it but was not sold on the idea. However, by the time dinner rolled around, I was free of the hangover feeling and 100% ready to party again that night. And so, I did.

Being concerned that I was probably going to flunk out and not do all the homework that was required, i.e., a paper that was due for a business class, I never attempted to start. One friend told me, "Just go to class every day, and the teacher will slide you with a D." I followed his ill-fated advice. Of course, it didn't work.

Once I returned home for the summer, I got my report card mailed to me. I think it showed I got four Fs and one D. I was also sent a letter from the college that I would not be accepted back. I felt humiliated. Now, what was I going to do? I was not going to give up on college, realizing I had done a really stupid thing by partying all that year. Oh, but I still must admit I did have a really great time but paid the ultimate price while, in hindsight, it was so immature of me. *AND*—how about all that money I wasted on tuition, rent, and board? Never would that happen as a responsible adult. Of course, I'm older and wiser now and not so young and naive anymore.

Third Year of College — Huge Reality Check

Now, it was time to get serious. It hit home hard what a stupid thing I had done the previous year. With my grade point average now almost worthless, no decent four-year school would accept me. I ended up enrolling in a junior college in northeastern Colorado.

I have always wanted to be famous since I was a kid. And in high school, after seeing *Smokey and The Bandit* and being a big fan of Burt Reynolds, I had thought of being an actor. I became a theater major, hoping this would be a stepping stone on the road that led to Hollywood. I took theater classes, such as set building and other related classes. The main classroom was to rehearse each trimester for a play. For one of the plays, the teacher selected a comedy that I did not find humorous.

I've never been a fan of live theater performances, as it's always been my contention that it's not how people respond or act in real life when it comes to blocking the play. It has always appeared to me that stage acting is too dramatic. I've always been of the belief that as an audience member, it should appear the lines have not been written and the actors are adlibbing as the story unfolds, just as people do in real-life conversations. I began taking issue with the blocking the teacher was making for the actors to follow when saying lines. To me, it came across as phony and not how things would unfold in real life. He did not listen to me as I was going for authenticity. Again, this is why I have never liked seeing a play. It comes across as choreographed and unnatural to me. Modern-day film acting seems to be much more realistic in how people react and behave in real life.

During the course of the first trimester of school that year, the theater teacher's daughter had returned home on her Christmas break from the college she was attending. She sat next to me in class during the rehearsal. We got to talking, and I became smitten, which I would later regret. For the next few weeks, we started dating, and again, I was falling fast for her. She became my first intimate experience with a woman. Having still the belief that one shouldn't have sex until marriage is a value I tried to hang onto. However, romantic passion got the better of me. A few things happened, but I still made sure things didn't go too far, fighting my temptations. The following day I felt cheap and guilty. I felt like a cheap street-level gigolo. She went back to college after her Christmas break was over. When our Christmas break came up, I had gone home. It did not go well with Mom. Mom and I were at each other's throats, arguing all the time. The day after Christmas, I went back to college and hung out for the remaining two weeks of Christmas break. The teacher's daughter and I stayed in touch, but soon after, it took a turn for the worse; she dumped me. The following year I wrote an angry poem about her. It was my way of telling her off and getting even.

During the winter trimester of drama class, the teacher said we had to put on a play for little grade school children. We were to make it up as a class and perform it together. I was thinking, *Are you kidding me! I did not sign up for this kind of acting.* I wanted serious actor training and work on a real play, not some *Romper Room* embarrassment. What came to fruition was a play where we all played animals, and it kind of had a *Wizard of Oz* theme. We performed it in the classroom, where we did the rehearsing. As I remember, it had to do with animals making friends as the first animal crawled on his hands and knees to each corner of the room, gathering up his newfound friends. I was designated to play a stupid dog. I was dressed up in some stupid costume to make me look like a dog with floppy ears. I also had to crawl around on the floor on my hands and knees, acting like a dog during the whole play. We had to perform that play *seven damn times!* I have never been so humiliated in my life!

I had dated only a couple of times that year. There was not much to choose from. I was able to get my GPA high enough that I got accepted to the University of Northern Colorado (UNC) in Greeley. The town was named for Horace Greeley, who's known for the famous quote, "Go west, young man." Ironically, he never set foot in Greeley. The thing I learned from my third year at college was that I no longer wanted to be an actor.

University of Northern Colorado

I would spend the next two and a half years attending UNC till I graduated at the end of the winter trimester of 1984. I had lost a lot of credits transferring around to three different colleges, which is one of the reasons it took me so long to obtain a degree. I'm thankful in a way that I flunked out. Because now it gave me the opportunity to list on my resume that I graduated from a university and not a po-dunk college. I loved every minute I spent at UNC. To me, this is what a real college is all about, and I miss those years. I made friends and had a good time socializing — a great experience.

After realizing I was not going to make it as an actor, I turned my focus back to a business major. Short-lived was that. Well, I attended a few days of business classes and realized it was over my head. I've also realized since then, over the course of getting to know myself all these years, I do not have a head for business. I have a head for creativity, such as drawing and writing a memoir, such as this, poetry, lyrics, and writing down my personal observations in life. I really enjoy writing and expressing what I have to say.

Once learning I was not going to succeed in obtaining a business degree, I quickly had to go through the course catalog and see what degree I thought I could achieve. I looked at all the course requirements to see what I could handle. I've always had a huge interest in politics since the time I was in grade school. My mom got me involved in helping her out on campaigns, and her interest rubbed off on me. UNC also required me to have a major and minor. I majored in geography and minored in political science.

While in my second year at UNC, I met the first person who I ever fell in love with. I fell fast and hard again. I really cared for her. I know I have mentioned past women, but up to this point, *Stacy* (not her real name) was truly the first one I wanted to seriously marry. Stacy was from a suburb of San Francisco. I think she chose UNC to become a teacher. UNC is primarily known for its big teaching program that produces teachers among other degrees, as well.

I first noticed Stacy walking through the mob of people changing classes. Every day we would pass each other. I began saying "Hi" to her, and she reciprocated. Having wanted to ask her out, I finally got the courage one day to ask her while we were passing each other. She said, "Yes." We went out a few times and even double-dated with Tim and his future wife, whom I once dated. In the short weeks that we had been dating, Stacy, while at my flat, informed me she had a boyfriend. I think they were in a rough patch and no longer were an official item. However, it was obvious Stacy still felt something for him.

Soon after that, I saw her on campus one afternoon and suggested we meet in the evening at the library to study. She had agreed to meet me. But something was off. She seemed distant and not so excited to see me. Anyway, the rest of the afternoon wore on, and that evening I went to the library, selected a table, and waited for her arrival. Well, she was not on time. Then a bit later, her roommate arrived with an envelope and gave it to me, saying something to the effect, "Stacy wanted me to give you this." Something was majorly wrong. I knew this spelled it was over. In that tainted envelope rests the second *Dear John* letter I received. It was approximately ten handwritten pages long and also basically stated she was going back to the relationship with her old boyfriend.

Right after reading that letter, I was totally devastated. Any chance of me trying to study that night was emotionally blown. I left the library having read that letter. I had never been hit that emotionally hard like this before over rejection. It upset me so much that I could not eat for three days. I did not hate her because she was fair, open, and honest with me. We stayed friends for a few years after that, and I sought dating advice, and she was more than happy to make suggestions. As a result, it spawned my favorite poem I ever wrote, How Many Times. *That* poem is written below. The bomb in that poem is a metaphor for her old boyfriend with whom she reestablished a relationship.

How Many Times

How many times does a heart have to break before it's beyond repair?
How many times must you sit and rot, waiting for the cure of time?
It seems like an incredible dream, but reality really existed.
Just yesterday, I was by her side; today, she doesn't recognize me.

I knew that she carried a bomb, but it exploded much too soon.
The hurt is still quite a surprise, but what an incredible dream it was!

Now, it's gone forevermore....
Love, it REALLY hurts!
There's got to be a solution to this painstaking madness!

How many times does a heart have to break before it's beyond repair?
How many times must you sit and rot, waiting for the cure of time?

How many times....
I ask you, how many times?

— WILLIAM C. DUCKWORTH
November 22, 1982

The first year I was at UNC, I had already known a few of the people there through my friend Tim, who started at UNC as a freshman. While attending the other college the previous year, occasionally, I would drive the two hours on a Friday for the weekend to UNC and party with friends Tim knew. Man, he had cool friends, and I bonded with them well. One of them that I hung out with was a Wild Man (whom I will refer to as for purposes of this book and not mention his name.) He'd do just about anything and was not afraid of a dare. Over the next couple of years, Wild Man did some crazy antics.

I had always wanted to do some crazy things that you hear stories about from others in your college years. Sometimes I'd be the instigator. Here are three such stories of many that bring a humorous smile to my face when I look back at them.

It was approximately around 9:30 on a warm spring night. There were three of us, and we were sitting outside finishing our meals at a chain fast-food restaurant that served tacos. Next door was a chicken fast-food restaurant. I suggested we play a prank on the workers in the drive-up window. "Let's drive up to the speaker and order all this food for the three of us, and then, after he's taken our order, suddenly change up our orders a few times and confuse the hell out of him."

My friends were game. We all loaded into Wild Man's car and did exactly what I proposed. Mind you, we never had any intention of eating what we ordered. Sure enough, we were confusing the order taker as we heard his voice coming from the speaker, "Are you guys for real?" We assured him we were, and when we were finally done placing this large order, we pulled around to the pickup window. When it came time for payment, Wild Man placed the paper bag full of garbage from our meals on the ledge. Wild Man said, "Ah, okay, here ya go." As soon as Wild Man did that, he peeled out of the drive-up lane as fast as possible onto the street. The three of us had a big laugh as we left the restaurant in the dust. However, we did not escape away swift and clean. The cashier had a quick reaction and was able to swat the bag of trash back inside Wild Man's car.

This event was not over yet. What happened next was completely Wild Man's idea. About twenty minutes had passed since we pulled our stunt. So, the Wild Man decided to go back and annoy the workers at the restaurant. It was somewhat late now with not much traffic. Wild Man drove back through the drive-through lane, past the order menu board and speaker, and pulled up to the pickup window. He stopped and honked his horn to get their attention. As soon as he did, he peeled out again, just like in a scene of the cartoon "The Road Runner and Wile E. Coyote." Well, it worked. One of the employees jumped in his car and began to follow us. So, now we were being chased. I remember that in an attempt to lose the guy, Wild Man quickly pulled into a cemetery at a high rate of speed. Just by pure luck, we did not hit any headstones. We may have lost the other guy for a moment, but the chase continued driving the nearby streets of Greeley, where the restaurant was located. Now, Wild Man was going fast, perhaps close to sixty m.p.h. through neighborhood streets with his lights turned off to try to lose the guy. At this point, I was getting scared. This prank was getting out of control and had gone beyond what I had proposed.

This next story was always fun to pull on people who didn't know me just to watch their reactions. When I was around Wild Man's friends who'd never seen me, I would talk like I came from an *extremely wealthy* family. We set his friends up at lunch in the cafeteria, and he would start off by asking me, "How is your dad's yacht doing?" I'd reply, "Well, it's currently being refurbished and upgraded with a nicer interior down in Miami, and we hope to cruise over to the Bahamas in it this summer." Then he'd ask me how my Mercedes was, and I'd reply, "Oh, my 380SL is ok, but I'm going home and switching it out. I'm gonna drive my mom's Jaguar. Yeah, she doesn't much care for it, as she thinks the Rolls Royce drives nicer. My dad's not happy about that because it's his Rolls, and now my mom wants it as her regular car. So, Dad's stuck driving the Maserati. Neither of my parents care much for that car. My dad would be driving the Bentley, but that's currently up at our mountain home in Vail." We had great fun as his friends would look at me with looks of, "Wow, his family must be so rich." I'd rattle off what I had to say so nonchalantly as if, "Isn't everybody this rich?" Wild Man would just keep feeding me questions, and I'd be adlibbing and elaborating on the spot.

The third story had to do with another of Wild Man's friends. Backstory: I have a pretty good British accent obtained from years of practice listening to British rock stars speak. Wild Man had this idea; he was going to invite this gal over while we were at his place to meet his new friend from England, who was also a student at UNC (me). I would talk in my British accent and adlib everything.

She came over and was excited to meet me. So, she asked me questions like how I ended up at UNC. I told her, in my cockney accent, "My dad, back in England, worked for an oil company and got transferred to Denver. Therefore, that's why I'm attending college in the States." I went on and on about stuff, and she was buying it "hook, line, and sinker." So, I decided to have a little more fun. I said I had been practicing my American accent and then talked normally; of course, she did not know that. Then I'd switch back to my cockney accent. Our conversation must have gone on for around twenty minutes. I did come clean, and Wild Man and I had a good laugh. We let the girl in on the joke, and she took it well and was not mad.

I spent one summer attending summer school. The reason was that I did not want to be around my mom. We were not getting along well. It also allowed me to graduate one trimester earlier. While at UNC, I found I could have a political internship for college credit, and that would knock off a big block of hours needed to complete the minor. I was able to get an internship in Washington, D.C., working for The Honorable William Armstrong, United States Senator from Colorado.

During my three months in D.C., I worked in different capacities within the office. Some of the work brought me face-to-face with some famous politicians. For example, on one occasion, I was walking down an empty hallway in one of the congressional buildings and was suddenly star-struck by the person walking toward me from the opposite direction. It was George McGovern. He ran against Nixon for President in 1972. I couldn't help but stare. As we passed each other, he smiled and said, "Hello," as did I. I think he may have been able to tell I was a bit starstruck. To top that, I just happened to stand in front of former-astronaut-turned-politician John Glenn. We were on a crowded escalator that was located underneath the Capitol building. I didn't dare speak to him as he was in conversation, likely with another congressman. I also once found myself in an elevator in the U.S. Capitol with T.V. network news correspondents Bret Hume and Bill Greenwood.

Because of my internship in D.C., I could see firsthand how the politicians are treated almost like royalty with all the perks that come with the job. It's no wonder why there are so many career politicians in D.C.

During my senior year, I met another girl I became smitten with at UNC. In fact, she was the second girl I fell in love with. She, too, was the type you'd want to bring home to your mother. She had that pure and innocent look to her. I had fallen hard and fast as I tended to do back in those days, but another *familiar* roadblock got in my way *AGAIN!* When I met her, she had just broken up with her boyfriend over Christmas break. He was not a college student but someone she met in high school, and they had been serious. Our relationship started out okay, but as the weeks rolled on, it came to an end, catching me off guard. It turns out she, too, got back together with her old boyfriend. Again, my heart was broken. That's when I received my third *Dear John* letter. That makes three in about a two-and-a-half-year span. I managed to stay in touch with her for a couple of years after I graduated. Still in love with her, she told me she was going to marry her boyfriend. I was so deeply in love with her that I seriously considered crashing the wedding, and when it came to the place where the officiant states, "Does anyone object to these two getting married? If so, speak now or forever hold your peace," that's when I was going to stand up and loudly say, *"I DO!"* I never did it or attended the wedding. Nor was I invited. That is how much I loved this woman at the time.

Prior to graduation, there was one more snag to overcome. UNC required you to write an essay. It had to be approved by two out of three English teachers. Thinking I knew what I was doing, I failed it five times. With assistance from an English teacher the sixth time, I passed it.

Finals week had arrived, and soon I'd finally be done with all my schooling. On my way home after my last final, I had planned a little personal celebration of rebellion. There was a popular song on the radio at the time by The Stray Cats, a rock-a-billy band. The song was "Sexy and Seventeen". There is a line that goes, "I ain't going to school no more." In the video, the singer is sitting at an old-fashioned school desk in a classroom. When he sings that line, he shoves his notebook, books, and papers on the floor out of defiance. I loved that image. When I got back to my apartment, the first thing I did was put on that song! Oh, it felt good!

I *finally* graduated from college! *NOW THIS WAS A BIG DEAL TO ME!* I was so proud of myself! It was a bearcat and a long haul to earn. After all the obstacles and having to make up those credits, I finally did it! It took five and a half years. I was twenty-five and in the Class of 1984.

Chapter 13

Thrown to the Wolves

What freedom I had to finally be finished with all my schooling. For the next two to three years, every time fall rolled around; I felt that nervousness of dreading school starting again, obviously what my gut was used to since first grade. Now, it was time to meet the real world and work till I retired around sixty-five, or so I thought that was the plan my future would take.

Having been a geography major prior to graduating, I had asked my advisor what type of job I could get with a major in geography and a minor in political science. He told me I'd probably be a good fit as a city planner. Hey, that sounded good. Thinking about the job might entail designing intersections and traffic lanes for more efficient traffic patterns. Who among us hasn't thought that while we're stuck in traffic, we could have redesigned the intersection and improved the timing of the lights better? Yeah, this sounded like it would be fun because I liked to draw and design things.

Well, the first thing I did was call the city and county of Denver's planning offices. I explained that I had just graduated with a geography degree and was inquiring about how I go about applying for a city planner job. The first question I was asked was, "What area of geography was my degree in?" *Uh-OH! I sense a bump in the road coming.* I replied, "It was just a general degree in geography." The person told me that I would have to go back to college and obtain a master's degree in a specialized area of geography, and then…get a job as a city planner in a small town and then work my way to the big city. *Oh.* I thought, being a bit shocked by the answer. I wasn't counting on all that. After my conversation, I said to myself, *I ain't going back to school. I just got done with all that, and it was a hassle.* Been there, done that. I made one more attempt with my geography degree and contacted a government office in Denver and tried to get on in the cartography department (map-making). That also turned out to be a no-go. I then turned to the world of politics using my connections I had made through networking and applied for a political position with the city of Denver. I exhausted those avenues, as well, that led nowhere.

Now, I had to reassess job searching and reach outside of my field of studies. I had landed an interview with a well-known luggage company. I felt it went fairly well, and the person who interviewed me took some interest. I could tell he was a bit hesitant and not quite sure about me being fresh out of college, but he did not turn me away. Instead, he gave me a description of the job duties for what he was hoping to hire. It was selling the well-known line of luggage to department stores. He suggested I go to a department store to look over the company's product lineup and see if I could truly sell it. I did just that, and I believe in the company and have owned pieces of its luggage. Yes, I could sell this with loyalty to the brand. I *wanted* this job. I went back and met with him again. Now, his mood had changed. The impression I came away with was that I was too green and not experienced enough for the position.

I made inquiries with different areas of the business world and was coming up empty-handed. Companies wanted experienced people and not rookies. I was getting frustrated because how do you get the experience if no one is willing to give you the work experience? I was, however, offered a job as assistant manager for a five-and-dime store. I thought about it and turned it down. I just didn't feel it was the right fit for me.

I finally found luck as a rental car agent. *Boy,* I thought. *This is it. A big corporation. I will stay with this company till I retire and move up the corporate ladder.* HA! Think again, Bill. The job turned out to be such a disappointment that I quit after six months. Once hired, I found out it paid minimum wage plus commission sales on the collision damage waiver (CDW) and the sale of medical coverage if the customer was injured in an accident. The rental company put extreme pressure on me to sell the CDW and medical coverage. They kept stats on me, and, at the end of each day, they reviewed each contract I wrote to see how much I sold. It worked like a grade point average.

They kept stats on all the employees' sales on a big sheet on the wall. You could compare how you were doing against your fellow co-workers. If you were lucky and most of your customers took it or you were able to talk them into taking the two coverages, you were doing well. However, most people choose not to take it. If you had a family renting a car for fourteen days and did not take any insurance that would ding you like getting an F when you had a 4.0 GPA. It would bring your stats way down, and it was hard to get them back up again. If you were *not* doing well, they would call you into the office and have a *sit-down,* mafia-style, and put pressure on me to go out there and sell it to the customers. This led the employees to project high-pressure sales onto the customers, and sometimes the customers would write to the corporate office and complain about the high-pressure sales tactics. Well, those contracts would get traced back to the rental agent, and then, once again, you would get hauled into the office and asked why did you piss off the customer? So, you couldn't win.

Employees started to lie to customers to increase sales. Some employees would say that their personal auto insurance would *not* cover the rental car. Actually, it does, and if the customer did not know that a lot of times, then some agreed to accept the insurance. Another tactic one guy used was to be fast with writing up the contract to sign and initial specific boxes. Since most people don't read contracts, they would just initial where they were told to do so. This one employee would circle that he wanted the insurance coverages, and he initialed without reading what he was signing. Boy, let me tell you when they returned the car, the charges would add up, and the bills were extremely expensive. They would complain. The assistant manager would end up getting involved and telling them, "Well, you initialed that you wanted it." After the customer realized he got tricked, he had no other choice but to pay for it.

Many customers left in disgust. (From my experience working this job, I have always been against commission sales as I saw firsthand how it promotes dishonesty.) Another trick some would use was if a customer told them his/her insurance did cover the rental car, the rental agent would grab the big computer printout that contained all the key codes; if a customer locked keys in the car, we could give them the key code to get a key cut that would open the door. Well, some would use the key code book, open it up and act like they were looking up to see if their insurance company covered it. "I'm sorry, but *such and such* company does not cover it." Ka-Ching. He/She just made another CDW sale.

This particular rental company also pulled a bait and switch. They advertised the smallest car they offered, and our location never provided that car. We had the next step up. Now, there was a secret other employees informed me about. Some of the rental cars may have problems. These were referred to as *D Mobiles*. The "D" stood for DECLINE, as in if someone declined to take the added insurance. The mechanics and/or the people who cleaned up the cars and who worked on them before they went back on the line would attach the keys to a piece of paper with a preprinted drawing of the front and back of the car (the purpose of this paper was to mark damage on the car before the customer drove off with it if they chose to decline the insurance.) When the car was ready to be put back on the line for another rental, if it had problems, they'd mark it up, such as flumes coming out of the grille, write "RENT ME" on the preprinted paper or even draw one to three stars that were code to us that the car *MAY* break down on them or might have trouble while they have the rental in their possession.

I'm an honest guy with a conscience, but a few times, I had to apply high-pressure tactics to customers to sell the CDW. The last straw was when I waited on a young mother and her two little children. I could tell they didn't have a big budget for their trip based on the comments the mother was making. Nevertheless, I got her to take the insurance. After that contract, I said to myself, *I can't keep ripping people off anymore*. My conscience bothered me too much, and I proceeded to give my notice.

The most I ever made at the rental car company was $600 in any one month during the six months I was there. One guy was making $30,000 a year, I was told, because of the way he cheated the customer and made the company money. There were other practices going on to cheat the customer. The duties of employees had to switch turns cleaning the bathrooms, and we were not allowed breaks. It was frowned upon if you took a seat during a lull when there were no customers. I thought about becoming a whistle-blower and reporting them to the state but thought there would be too much blowback, and I didn't want any negative attention coming my way.

Having left the rental car world, I was at a loss for which job or industry to tackle next. I had gone to the library to the reference section and pulled out a book on different careers and requirements for those jobs. I found that insurance companies would hire you as long you had a degree, no matter what it was in. After interviewing with a few companies, I found one that hired me to be an adjuster.

I started off as an in-house adjuster, handling non-injury car accidents and determining who was at fault. To my surprise at such a young age of twenty-six, was all the pushback and flack I receive from people who did not like my determination of whom I deemed at fault. After doing a complete investigation, I thought after my training when I was thrown to the wolves to handle actual claims with real people, that it would be much like *The Peoples' Court*. People would accept my decision as final. They'd think, *Well, you're the insurance man. I guess you know best.* Not even close! Man, I dealt with some really angry people, who swore at me, and even in one case, I had our insured threaten to sue me if I paid the claim, and the claimant threatened to sue me if I didn't pay the claim. Being an insurance adjuster is a thankless job that wears you down to the point of burnout. I almost needed combat pay to attract me to stay.

While there, I was still living at home for OCD reasons, and some evenings, I would come home so stressed out and convey to my mom what a bad day I had. I was looking for support and taking my side, she did the opposite and took the insurance company's side. She would say about the people who got mad at me, "It's not you they're mad at. It's the insurance company they're mad at." *Hogwash!* It was *ME* personally who denied their claim, not the insurance company! She would also side more times with the insurance company and *not* take my side and say, "Work harder" or "Talk to your Supervisor." *HA! Talk to my Supervisor? That shows I can't handle the job. This is not like junior high when you have problems in school and go to talk to your counselor. Thanks, Mom; you're a big help, facetiously speaking.* I lasted only six years, and then I flat out couldn't deal with it anymore and quit.

While at the insurance company, some *MAJOR* things happened to me. There was a woman co-worker who started work there two years after I did. I fell in love with her, and in the long run, she ended up metaphorically stabbing me in the back. She sent me into a downward spiraling—falling into the worst suicidal depression I had ever known. I had hit *MY* rock bottom. It would take me till 2016 before I could get over her or should I say to the point that she wasn't constantly on my mind. It took me many, many years to become emotionally well again. (More on that in the next chapter.)

There were other situations that caused me major embarrassment all due to my OCD. I had to keep silent about my OCD. It was circa 1986, and the term obsessive compulsive disorder was a fairly new term that not many people knew about. Now, it's become household knowledge at the sound of the term being thrown around today, and most people have a gist of the bare basics of it.

A few years into the job, I switched over to being an auto adjuster. I went to tow lots and body shops to evaluate damaged or totaled vehicles. The perk of this position was that we were given our own company car to drive and were able to take it home at night. Let me first say in my mind that there is nothing dirtier on this planet than feces. Quite often, I would be required to visit tow yards. These cars were towed from the accident scene.

The protection these tow yards used were *Junkyard dogs* that lived there 24/7. As a result, they would crap all over the grounds, and it would not be picked up. Obviously, with OCD, this freaked me out. Sometimes, I would accidentally step in it. Other times, whenever possible, I would lay my briefcase on a nearby car and get out the needed forms. On occasion, I would not be able to put my briefcase on anything and would be forced to lay it on the ground–sometimes near the feces from the dogs. Having OCD made me fear that even though the briefcase did not touch the feces, it might as well have. See, in my *doubting mind,* one of the symptoms of OCD made me think that I could just assume the briefcase touched the feces. As a result, driving back to the office, having the fear of contamination from my bare hands, handling the briefcase made me feel as if they were covered with feces. So, I drove with tissues placed over the steering wheel where I'd put my hands.

Once I returned to the office, I threw the tissues on the back seat floor. With no trash can nearby, and because of the total fear of contamination that I would transfer from my hands to the tissues (so bad I'd want to change clothes sometimes and would have the need to wash my hands for three minutes.) It was simply easier and less emotionally stressful, to let the tissues build up. After a while, the back floor was completely filled with loose pieces of tissue that began to overflow to the height of the lower back seat door to door. I kept the briefcase on the back seat while driving, thus contaminating the back seat, and I sure as hell would not want to sit where I had placed the briefcase. That part of the seat was now filthy (in my OCD mind), having spread the feces from the briefcase to the back seat.

One day while working in the office, I happened to be the lone adjuster with a company car while the other adjusters were out in the field. The manager of the office came up to me and needed use of my car as he had to visit an attorney's office on company business. This is where OCD screwed me over again. I was now suddenly frightened as he was going to see what condition the interior of the car was in and his reaction. I sweated it out until he returned to the office. Once he returned, I learned my fate. He had my supervisor meet him in his office. For a minute there because he did not comment to me about the appearance of the interior of the car, I thought I may have dodged a bullet. Not even after a few minutes, my supervisor approached and informed me I would temporarily lose the privilege of the company car for personal use. I would now have to leave the company car at the office and drive my own car to and from work. Then, I would pick up the company car to do my assignments. It was embarrassing that night as my supervisor had to take me home in his personal car. The whole office of twenty-six people knew what happened to me. Before I went home that afternoon, I was instructed to take the company car and go to the car wash, have it vacuumed out, clean the interior, and throw all the trash away. In my manager's and supervisor's eyes, it appeared to them that I disrespected the privilege of having a company car and that I had just trashed the interior by not clearing out the amount of garbage accumulated. That was the farthest thing from the truth. I could not tell them of my OCD problem as I would look crazy in their eyes that I had a fear of contamination. In fact, just a year before, I had met with another psychiatrist about washing my hands so often and explaining to him my fear of contamination.

Up to this point in my life, I thought it was just me with this life-altering fear of contamination condition. After explaining it to the psychiatrist, he then suddenly told me I have OCD. "OCD what?" I asked. Then he explained to me the medical condition and told me other people have it, as well. I felt relieved. It was right around the mid-1980s when OCD was finally given a proper diagnosis and named obsessive compulsive disorder. I felt a degree of relief now, learning I was not the only one with crazy thoughts going through my head. Before meeting with this psychiatrist and learning of OCD while working at the insurance company, I was being so mentally tormented by it that I was giving myself deadlines by setting a date. If I could not make myself better by trying hard not to wash my hands, I would kill myself. I so wanted to be free of OCD. If I were dead, then I'd be at peace and not have to deal with the dreadful OCD. Yes, OCD was that out-of-control, dominating my life in everything I did. Those dates came and went. I guess I did not have the nerve to kill myself. After many months, I was given back the privilege of being able to take the company car home again.

I was also bullied by my previous supervisor and manager in my office. Another factor with OCD that happened at the insurance office was the use of the men's restroom. Now, in between the sink was a small vertical partition that separated the sink from the urinal. Well, after about a year of washing my hands in the sink next to the urinal, my OCD doubts started creeping in and taking over my mind and made me start thinking where I went to place my hands inside the urinal after washing my hands before I reached for the paper towel that was located near the urinal. (This may sound completely absurd to a person *who is not* afflicted with OCD, but let me tell you, a person with OCD would understand completely what I'm talking about and the stress it causes.) So, instead of washing my hands in the restroom, I would go to the breakroom and wash my hands there. I would stand there washing my hands for two-three minutes. (I must feel totally clean and be SURE of it before I stop.) Well, it was obvious I could no longer hide the fact that I had a hand-washing problem and that I could not tell people why because they would not understand it. After a few months, the female supervisor I had at one time was leaving the breakroom while I was washing my hands and made a snide remark on her way out, "Are you finished with your *BATH?*" *What a Bitch!* I thought.

Before I tell you how my manager of the claim's office bullied and embarrassed the hell out of me, let me give you a little backstory. I tried to be very professional in the way I dressed. It had been a few years since having graduated college. I tried to dress sharply. I wore suits and nice dress shoes. I was doing the *GQ (Gentlemen's Quarterly* magazine) look. I saw the movie *Wall Street* with Charlie Sheen, and I started slicking my hair back to get that same look. I had also recently purchased a new 1986 Bronco II. I outdressed every male in the office. I appeared successful, and I think some of my co-workers were jealous, based on some snide remarks and judgments made toward me. I did have some independent money obtained from the death of my biological parents, so I didn't always cash my paychecks in a timely fashion. That turned out to be a mistake.

One day, while I was working at the drive-in where people who had drivable cars would bring them to our office, out of the blue, I was blindsided by my manager (whom I believe hated me). He came to my desk in the drive-in, and in front of my co-workers and customers, waiting for their estimates, he had a hat filled with small pieces of cut-up paper and said in front of me so everyone could hear, "Bill, we're all drawing numbers to see who gets your paychecks since you don't cash them." I was livid! However, I could not show that and had to artificially play along with the joke and force an insincere laugh. Who would do such a thing in front of everyone when it's my *PRIVATE* business when I cash my checks? Why did that bastard manager make a fool of me in front of people? I think that was his intention. When I got a free moment, I went and asked him how he knew that I did not cash my paychecks in a timely manner. He informed me that the regional office had called him to see why I wasn't cashing them. Apparently, it was messing up their bookkeeping. My thought then was, *Why didn't the person at the regional office contact me directly?* That I will never know, but I think it shows a lack of tactlessness on behalf of the regional office. I think my manager got a big kick out of embarrassing me in front of customers and my co-workers. I thought seriously of calling the regional office and talking to the second or third in command and making a formal complaint against my manager. In the end, I decided against that as it would make me look like a disgruntled employee and could hurt my chances for advancement.

Being an adjuster was very stressful. The phone was constantly ringing, and calls would take on average ten to fifteen minutes to handle the matter at hand, whether you were dealing with an angry agent who didn't want you to pay the claim of his/her insured, negotiating with body shops needing more labor time added to the estimate to complete the repairs, and taking recorded statements from an insured or claimant on his/her version of the story to see how the accident unfolded.

After about six years, I was really getting burnt out as an adjuster, and I really couldn't take much more of it. I was not cut out for that job. It was so highly stressful that it crossed my mind that I might have had a heart attack. I thought the stress would be good for burning calories as I was starting to put on weight. Years later, I found out stress creates cortisone, which makes you fat. There goes that theory out the window for trying to lose weight. Work got so bad that I was becoming buried in paperwork, and I started to clash with my supervisor and manager. I was getting thirty calls in an eight-hour day. No joke, because I counted the number of phone messages. That worked out to be one phone call every fifteen minutes. On more than one occasion, as my work required me to be out in the field on most days, I usually couldn't get back to the office till around noon. The bottom line was that the insurance company did not hire enough claims adjusters to handle the claim volume. As a result, customer service suffered. Due to the pressure and the stress, I was beginning to fall behind as my workload stacked up. That resulted in my being put on probation, the kiss of death, which meant the company was now looking for a reason to fire me. I had no future there. Therefore, I gave my notice. I had given it my all. I did that job to the best of my ability and had worked close to a fifty-hour week.

Chapter 14

Danger Zone — Playing with Fire

How many times does a heart have to break before it's beyond repair? There is a part of my soul that will always be saddened that contains my *biggest* regret. In my case, regret has both positive and negative connotations.

I have never found anyone to love me in a legitimate relationship. One of the things in life that has always bothered me is that I have never experienced a truly lasting romantic sexual relationship. I envy those who have. I am in the minority when it seems like a cakewalk for everyone else. I wish I knew the secret everyone else has learned in finding that lasting relationship. As for me, I'm still searching for the answer to that secret, and I'm running out of time.

I'm sixty-four at this writing, and I've lost count of how many women I've asked out or gone out with. However, it must be around sixty. The number of women I've asked out far outweighs the number of dates I've been on. Not one successful long-term relationship came from all the effort and energy I invested. I would think the odds would be in my favor. They say it's a numbers game. Well, not so much in my case. Upon reflection, going back and looking over all the years and the money I've spent on dating women, traveling to meet them, online dating, speed dating, attending dinner groups, taking singles' cruises, taking dating classes, sending flowers, attending singles' events, making long-distance phone calls, and giving gifts, etc., I bet it adds up close to $10,000, and nothing came from it. It's emotionally exhausting.

Questions and Answers of Loneliness (by me, 1983)

Q. What price must be paid for loneliness?
A. There's not a price–you just suffer the cost.

A. I never asked for such silent loneliness.
T: One never asks for it–it's just dealt to you.

Q. Then how the hell do you get away from it?
A. One doesn't; only time will tell if you will graduate from it.

Q. Then I must suffer the cost until time is on my side?
A. Yes, but for some people, time is always against them.

The closest I've ever come to a legitimate relationship lasted one month. She went back to her ex-husband. That seems to be a recurring theme for me. The ones I choose seem to dump me and go back to their ex-husbands or old boyfriends. The amount of rejection I've faced makes me feel as if I repel women, just like a can of bug spray.

When I worked at the insurance company, I developed a crush on a new hire who was married. I will call her Gertrude. The year was 1987. She resembled a young Julie Andrews, and we were the same age. She had that wholesome, girl-next-door look, the sweet innocence of a young Doris Day. It's obvious why I was so taken with her. I did not *dare* make a move toward this *married* lady. However, every day, without fail, I checked to see if she wore her wedding ring. For, if it were missing, it may indicate trouble in paradise, and her marriage could be over. That never happened. Two years went by, and my crush on her never waned. I continued to ask women out. The following is my recollection of knowing Gertrude.

In 1989, the insurance company held a profit-sharing dinner. It was held at a swanky restaurant, and as everyone was being seated at a circular table that donned white tablecloths, I held off trying to position myself to sit next to Gertrude. I was successful in doing so.

After dinner, when most were going home, I hung around where people were getting their coats, hoping to get a moment alone to compliment her. When the moment was right, I told her that I thought very highly of her. She was graciously pleased and smiled. I think she responded kindly. Then, her husband showed up, and she introduced me to him.

A few days went by. Now, back at work, I asked her if she would like to go to lunch, and she accepted. I felt this *could* be wrong, but then I justified it by asking myself, *What could a harmless lunch do?* At lunch, we seemed to hit it off. I sensed that she had an attraction toward me. I asked her if she would like to have lunch again, and she said something to the effect, "I just don't want to make a habit of it." So, I did not pursue it as I was developing feelings for her that went beyond a crush. *I could be headed into dangerous territory,* I thought, so I just let things be.

Weeks had passed since we had lunch, and Gertrude started to make small overtures toward me. One of the perks I enjoyed was the fact I often had to pass the desk of her co-worker, who was a friend of Gertrude's who sat next to her. As I passed her friend's desk, I always looked over to catch a glimpse of Gertrude. Her co-worker started to pick up on this. Her friend would make eye contact with me, give me a suspicious smile, and sometimes roll her eyes in Gertrude's direction. She knew our secret.

One Friday evening, I worked late, trying to catch up on the endless paperwork. After a good forty-five minutes from the time everyone left, Gertrude popped into the office dressed casually. She informed me that she had forgotten her paycheck. She stuck around for approximately thirty minutes, and we chit-chatted. Months later, she admitted she wanted to make dinner for me that night. WOW!

While still at the office one afternoon, my phone rang. It turned out to be Gertrude's friend who sat next to her. She asked if I had checked my office mailbox. Having said no, I immediately went to check and found two small pieces of candy. I grabbed them and put them in my mouth. I thought they were from the receptionist, whom I thought was interested in me as we had some friendly banter. Later, I came to find out they were placed there by Gertrude. *Okay, this is getting interesting, but because she is married, this is not what married women do.* Gertrude was taking a sincere interest in me. I felt an uncomfortable yet exciting feeling that felt so extreme. For the first time, I was not having to put in all the effort.

I started to test her and park my car in a few different spots as I pulled in every morning to see if she parked next to me. Each time she *did* park next to me. This helped me confirm that she was serious about me.

More weeks went by. One early Friday afternoon, she asked if I wanted to meet on a nearby grassy hill and just talk after work to get to know each other better. I said, "Yes," knowing now I was starting to step over the line. Just the chance to talk to my crush was too tempting for me to turn down. It was a very innocent meeting of enjoyable conversation.

Once, I was working in the drive-in (where people drove their damaged cars to us) at a rare moment when I was alone. Suddenly, I was surprised when Gertrude appeared, handing me a greeting card in an envelope. She did not utter a word and left. The look on her face was that of seduction. Something I call *Love Eyes*. The only time I have ever seen that look on women is when passion is involved. I thanked her and wondered, *Why is she giving me this? Married people don't do this.* Obviously, I could not wait to open it. It was a nice friendship-type card with some pre-printed semi-romantic phrase with her handwritten note that read something to the effect, "I hope we can become better friends." Wow, that threw me. I knew now she liked me romantically. Was she looking to start an affair? I knew now she took the basic plutonic level of friendship and bumped it up a notch.

A few more weeks went by, and she called me on a Friday afternoon at my extension and asked if I wanted to meet again. Sure, of course I did. We drove *our* cars to that same grassy hill, but this time, we parked side by side, and she jumped into the passenger seat of my car. Again, nothing happened, but that's about the time I found out she had a crush on me, too, for the last two years, and sitting next to each other at the profit-sharing dinner was no accident. She informed me that she was also trying to sit next to me. Two minds unknowingly had worked together at the same time. I had no idea she had a crush on me back then. She had told me that when she first saw me, I was the most handsome man she had ever seen. WOW, what a boost to my ego.

For weeks and months after that, we met in my car at the same location every Friday after work. It was clear we both felt strong feelings for each other — still, I had never even touched her yet because she *was married*.

Now, the guilt was really starting to set in. I knew what I was doing was wrong, but I could *not* help myself as I was not even on cloud nine. I was on cloud twenty-nine. She made me feel so good about myself. This was an exuberant feeling that I'd never known. And for the first time, I had a woman that was sincerely interested in me. Another time, we decided to meet after work on a Friday evening. We met at a bar, and we each had a well-known Mexican beer. After a bit of conversation, out of the blue, she said, "I care for you." Now, she took it up another notch, *again*.

I went on vacation that fall to Great Britain (GB). Gertrude was on my mind constantly, and I was missing her. I believe I was in love with her by this time but still had never touched her as she was *still* a married woman, and I was fighting my morals that I couldn't touch a married woman. Before I left for GB, I hatched a plan in my mind that I was going to show her how much I cared for her and tried to impress her by calling from GB. It was a challenge with the British operator trying to place a credit card call, but after a few difficult minutes, the call went through. Gertrude was surprised. It was an expensive $80 call for about twenty minutes, but to me, it was worth every penny.

I had gone on vacation circa the early 1990s to Florida as I was considering moving to a warmer climate as I detest Colorado winters. I even made it to Key West. Before I left Key West, I had called Gertrude from my hotel room as a surprise and let her know where I was. I had told her that if she had been there with me, we would probably never have made it out of the hotel room. On the way back toward the mainland of Florida, I stopped at a seashell shop on a Key and picked out a nice seashell. I had it gift-wrapped, *especially* for Gertrude.

When I returned from my vacation, Gertrude was a great sight for sore eyes. We knew we'd be meeting up that coming Friday night in my car. By this time, these meetings were now lasting until 10 or 11 p.m. I did ask her, "Don't you think your husband might get suspicious?" She replied, "I'll just tell him I went to the show or out with friends." After work, I got to the parking lot where we always met. I had a Ford Bronco II at the time. It had a cubby hole built into the dash right above the glove box. I put the gift-wrapped seashell in the cubby hole and threw a towel over the hole to cover up the surprise gift. Once she hopped in my car, we exchanged a few pleasantries. Then I said, "Oh, can you hand me that towel?" As she removed that towel, she saw her gift. She liked it. That's when I produced the plastic champagne glasses and the non-alcoholic simulated champagne. I made a toast to us and told her we must interlock our arms around each other's as if we were celebrating our wedding. As the evening went on and it became dark, I asked her if I could hold her hand. Fearing she might reject the offer (I had been rejected in college by a woman when I put my arm around her at the movies, and she took my arm and put it back by my side), Gertrude responded, "Can't you feel me willing you to?" I reached out and grabbed her hand. Shortly thereafter, we then shared our first kiss. Then she rested her head upon my lap and said she felt safe with me and that she "felt fifteen again." Nothing beyond kissing happened that night.

After a few more rendezvous meetings, things escalated a little further. As we kissed passionately, she said, out of the blue, "Stop me if I go too far." I won't mention what happened, far from what you may imagine. At the end of the night, Gertrude began to cry and felt confused. We had crossed a line that night. She was tearful because she had broken her wedding vows.

At this point now, my guilt began to eat away at me like the flesh-eating virus. I was now becoming conflicted and not sure she was *The One* for me. That created a bit of a rift in our relationship. I started to pull back a little and became a tad distant. Originally, when we first started meeting, I wanted to marry her, but now, since we were pretty hot and heavy, I started doing some soul-searching. At that time, U2 had a hit on the radio, "I Still Haven't Found What I'm Looking For." I really identified with that song and my situation at that point in time.

At a time when I was feeling confused during the dark turn my romantic life had taken, Gertrude and I had made previous plans to go out to dinner and to a bookstore. I wanted to buy her a book on GB; having traveled there, I wanted to share the love I have for GB with her. Mind you, this was planned for our traditional Friday night meet-up. When that Friday rolled around, we were not in the best place, as I was a bit distant from dealing with the guilt that was eating me alive. Gertrude arrived at work wearing a high-class, two-piece blue dress. She looked beautiful. I had never seen her so dressed up before. As the day progressed, I was going back and forth in my mind if we should make such an *official date* that was so morally wrong. By 4 p.m., I had decided to go through with it. We left her car in a nearby restaurant parking lot so it would be out of sight of the workplace lot. We always tried to avoid being discovered by our coworkers that we were having an affair. I'm pretty sure they knew anyway.

Having arrived at the bookstore, I selected a book on Ireland that contained beautiful pictures of the hamlets and countryside. She was pleased, and off to dinner we went. I had not told her where we were going as I wanted it to be a surprise. We arrived at a prestigious athletic club where I was a member. Not only was it a workout facility; in addition, it had a very nice dining room with white tablecloths. As we walked into the building, she said, "Well, Bill, you've got me outclassed." After dinner, we drove back to the parking lot we always met at on Friday evenings. On the way, she again rested her head on my lap.

Once we arrived, a bit of passionate kissing ensued when, out of the blue, she said, "I want to make love to you." Well, that was the first night I had ever been fully intimate with a woman. I must have been in my late twenties. After that, we had very few passionate nights like that due to the secrecy and difficult timing of planning when to get together. I was still doing my best to hold back because she was married, and it was wrong.

Because I was so deeply involved emotionally in this relationship, it was consuming me, and I was racked with guilt. I thought about her all the time. I hated the weekends because I had to go for two days without laying eyes on her. She was the last thing I thought about before I went to sleep and the first thing I thought about when I woke up. Gertrude and I had talked about us getting together for real. She had a son who was around five or six. She said she'd have to wait until he turned eighteen.

I started to tell my immediate family about the affair one by one at separate times. Partly out of guilt, I needed to confess that I was not acting in an appropriate manner and partly because I wanted them to know I'd met the love of my life. I told my sister first, and she said that most woman who have affairs will never leave their husbands. That kind of shocked me because of the strong bond Gertrude and I shared. It turns out my sister was right in the end. Then I let my dad know next. This was more of a confession. I was living in an isolated world where I could not tell anyone for it was wrong. After informing my dad, he told me to break it off and get out of the situation. He said, "You gotta think about what you're doing to her husband." He was absolutely correct; however, I did not have the strength to do it. I was too much in love with Gertrude, and I was feeling something that I *had never felt before.* The only other people I had let know I was having an affair were two of my friends. At around age twenty-seven *for* the first time in my entire life, I had a woman who legitimately loved me; I knew she loved me when things were good because we were both intensely interested in each other. I felt completely comfortable with her. If I were to list everything I desired in a woman, she would be it and much more. I was so deeply, deeply in love with her that it was beyond what words can describe.

Not long after our official date, I became so burnt out as an adjuster that I just couldn't take the requirements of the job anymore. I was at my wit's end. I had given four weeks' notice. I was on probation and working my tail off. I was not a slacker. We were so understaffed, and I was swamped. After roughly six years, I was free from the insurance company.

I still lived at home at the time, mainly because OCD had such a stranglehold over me that I would need reassurance from my mom if I felt contaminated or needed to wash my hands. Mom would be there to reassure me. Let me reiterate: OCD causes you to doubt and cloud your judgment, and Mom was there with the reassurance I needed, who thought logically, which saved me time by not having to wash my hands over and over. I needed to take a good six to seven months off. I needed time away from such a stressful job. I needed time to do some soul-searching, not only to figure out my next move in life, but also to evaluate my situation in dealing with the guilt of the affair.

I cannot begin to describe in words how badly the guilt was killing me inside. The affair I was having did not reflect my true character. I have always been an honest person with very high morals, yet I had dipped down to behaving in a mischievous manner to the low-level status of men who cheat on married women. *Ah, but since I am single, am I grouped in with the cheaters? Or am I a man who is having an illegitimate relationship with a woman who is cheating on her husband? So, is she the lone cheater?*

In Gertrude's eyes, I could do no wrong. In fact, she wrote me a love letter, and in it, she described me as her knight in shining armor. Wow, what an ego boost. The emotions I was feeling clouded my better judgment, and the passion got the better of me.

I'd been unemployed for approximately one month, and now I felt I had to come clean to my mom. I was literally scared to death to tell my mom that I was having an affair. But at this point, I was at a loss how to rectify my guilt. I was feeling so fearful of my mom's reaction. I literally felt she would probably disown me or cut me out of her will. So, I just ripped the bandage straight off the guilt-ridden emotional wound and told her straight out, "Mom, I'm having an affair." Shocking to me was her response. "You think you're the first person without sin to cast the first stone?" She spoke. She was not mad at me at all. She could tell that what I had confessed took much courage and that it was difficult to admit. I had then let her know that's why I stayed out so late on Friday nights. She responded, "I had a feeling something like that was going on." My mother obviously did not approve of the affair, but she was there for me, and for only the second and last time in my life, she took my side and understood the emotional pain I was dealing with. I also told her the guilt was eating me alive inside and that I wanted to do the right thing and break it off.

The next morning around 9 a.m. I called Gertrude. As soon as she answered, I was just frank and to the point that I had to break it off to do the right thing. She said verbatim, in an angry, upset voice, and I quote, "Don't worry about me; I'll be fine!" And that was basically all there was to the phone call. I felt relieved and sad at the same time, and I felt for her. It turns out my heart could not let her go.

Six weeks later, I couldn't stand not talking to her; while still thinking about her and missing her immensely, I called her at the office. I explained that I could not live without her, and asked if we could reconnect and start over. In a mild, angry response, she replied, "I tried really hard these last six weeks to work on my marriage." I thought, *Oh no! It's not going to happen.* But, by the end of the call, she was willing to start over.

We talked often by phone for the next few months—no meeting in person. I ended up getting a job with a credit union not terribly far from the insurance office, and our Friday night meetups in my car resumed. Intimacy did not happen very often at all. It was mainly kissing and catching up. However, we were getting to know each other so well that at times, there were disagreements over politics and other issues.

When we reached sticking points in the relationship, we were never able to discuss them fully to resolve them because, unlike legitimate couples, we had such limited time to work it out since we were sneaking phone calls to each other. At times, all that was allotted was leaving voice mails back and forth, and when we did meet, there was little time to resolve things. This put a big strain on the relationship, and cracks were developing.

By now, it was around 1992. This time, *she* decided *she* wanted to end it. Despite our differences, I was now 100% sure Gertrude was my soulmate. She was the one! I had never ever connected emotionally and on so many other levels with someone like her before. Our kisses went together like two perfectly matched jigsaw puzzle pieces. It was as if our lips planted together were a custom-made fit.

I was devastated, and that's putting it mildly. I fell into a deep, deep depression for many years to follow. My days became gray and grim. I would get up and go to my job. I would sit and eat my lunch in my car as my depression crushed me. I had lost my appetite. I was just eating minimally. When I arrived home from work, I'd go straight to bed without eating supper. Then, I repeated the process over the coming months. After several weeks, Mom started feeling rejected by me and felt I no longer wanted to eat dinner with her anymore. It wasn't that at all. I had lost my appetite, and life had lost all purpose for living. I was just trying to get through life as best I knew how at that time. I had basically hit rock bottom with my depression. I was feeling so alone and rejected. Life had no purpose anymore. Yes, I was considering suicide. If I had chosen suicide, I could have taken myself out of the emotional pain and set myself free. I had lost all reason to live.

Before Gertrude dumped me, I was always in good spirits around the office. I was always playing practical jokes on co-workers and lighting up the workday, making it more enjoyable. When I fell into the deep depression, my personality started to change. I was no longer that happy guy who played jokes and interacted with coworkers. My personality became somber and withdrawn. I just kept to myself, did my job, and went home. Coworkers started to notice I was withdrawing, and several people asked if I were okay. I lied and said yes.

The following quote is taken from a poem I wrote on February 14, 1983, and describes my mental state at the time perfectly: "I appear to contain a contented shell. But on the inside, I'm depressed as hell." I couldn't talk to anyone at work about what was going on in my private life.

In the fourth chapter, I described how my mom was obsessed with cleaning. She expected me to get up at 8 a.m. and clean till late afternoon on both Saturday and Sunday. When I became so depressed over Gertrude, I was *defiant* over getting up. One Saturday, I refused to get up and stayed in bed all day due to my heartbreak over Gertrude. Oh boy, did that set my mom off! She got extremely mad at me because I refused to get up. She kept coming to my room at least five times over the course of the day, demanding I get up, and I refused! It got her very agitated with me. Finally, around 4 p.m., she came in. She was sympathetic (she knew Gertrude had dumped me and why I was so depressed) and said, "Bill, what can I do to help you?" I responded, "Just make Gertrude like me again."

This mode of my lifestyle lasted for many months. The degree of my depression had turned so bad it prompted my mom to ask me if I wanted to be hospitalized for depression. I hesitated for a moment, then turned her down. At this point, I was more or less living in bed. I would only leave my bed to eat, shower, use the bathroom, and go to work. I had heard the expression, "He died of a broken heart." I thought it meant someone just missed someone very much. However, being in such a depressive state, I started to believe *I might actually die of a broken heart.* I cannot begin to tell you the emotional pain I was feeling. It was indescribable. I had lost the one and only love of my life that I felt was perfect for me. When things were good between us, it was the greatest feeling I had ever experienced. I had never felt that way about a woman before. I have never felt that way about a woman since.

Then one morning while driving to the credit union after many, many months without communication with Gertrude, we happened to notice each other's cars on the highway. (For a short distance, we took the same highway to get to our jobs.) I ignored her out of anger. As she exited an off-ramp, I saw her waving to me. I did not wave back. I continued my way to work and thought nothing of it. When I got to my desk that morning, my phone was blinking. I listened to the message. It was Gertrude. She was glad to see me on the highway.

Well, it was both good and bad to hear from her. Yes, I liked it, but now she was playing with my feelings again. That was bad. Obviously, now I started to think about her again, but I stayed strong and did not return the phone call. It may have been the next day, but when I returned from lunch, there was a bouquet of yellow flowers sitting on my desk with a small envelope attached. It caught me off guard as I had no idea who would have sent me flowers. I opened the envelope and the card read "From your brown-eyed girl." Gertrude had brown eyes, but there was a double meaning to her note. We were both big fans of Jimmy Buffett, and she was referring to Jimmy Buffett's cover version of Van Morrison's "Brown Eyed Girl".

Now I was mad! After discovering they were from her, I did not want them at all! No way. No how! She had burned me big time. So, I immediately tried to give them away to any female co-worker who wanted them. I had no takers. I think they were surprised that someone who was thoughtful enough to send me flowers was why I didn't want them. I think I told the women in the office there that they were from a girl who dumped me, and I didn't like her anymore and wanted to trash them. Yes, after no takers, I set them down next to my trash can, hoping the janitor would throw them out. I ended up letting my mom have them after letting her know who they were from. The following day, I got a call from Gertrude asking if I had received the flowers. She must have been dying, sitting on pins and needles, waiting for my call to say thank you. That call never went out. I said I did, and thank you. But I was not super friendly toward her. Well, somehow, after that call, our relationship was back on. But we did not meet very often after that. But I called her every day of the workweek.

As the years went on, there were other on-again, off-again times of just communication. At one time I was at another job after the credit union and called her every lunch hour from a pay phone. On one of those calls, she said something I always found endearing. She had mentioned that she depended on my calls every day. We were in a great place again, and I was back on cloud 29, although we were not meeting up anymore as our job locations made it impractical.

By now, I was living in an apartment. She came over a few times. So, we decided to make an official rendezvous at my apartment, where she would come over in the evening. Consider it an in-house date.

The date was November eighth in the late nineties. I remember it in detail as if it happened just last night. It was our first official night of passion. I had planned a romantic evening. I was dressed up in khakis, a dress shirt, tie, along with a blue blazer and dress shoes. This was going to be a *special* night. When she arrived, she looked dazzling, like I'd never seen her before. She had her hair all fixed up nicely and corkscrew curls coming down on each side of her face. She was dressed in a full-length green dress with buttons that started at the top and continued down the full length of the dress. She was a mind-blowing sight for me to see.

I had alcohol libations and poured her a glass. Then I put on Linda Ronstadt's song, "I've Got a Crush on You" from the Nelson Riddle Orchestra album. We slowly embraced and danced around my living room. Then I put on K.D. Lang's song, "Constant Craving", and we slow danced to that, too. The night blossomed into full bliss and still remains the most romantic night I've ever spent with a woman.

Some months after that, her son finally turned eighteen. I held Gertrude to her word from years earlier. I pressed her if she would get a divorce. She told me now that they had been a family for so long that there were too many memories shared together, and she couldn't part from the unit she had. 1-? Another strikeout. Crash and burn, baby. It wasn't pretty.

Soon after I moved into my townhouse, as our contact with each other was dwindling again. One night I got creatively romantic and decided to call her work number and left her a voicemail of me serenading her acapella style to "Love Me Tender". I never got a response. I'm willing to bet she never listened to it and just deleted the message.

As more time passed, I did not hear from her when my birthday rolled around, and I was hoping to get a birthday card from her. In previous years at times, she had remembered my birthday. My birthday came and went; I heard nothing. That stung. That night I left her a voice mail on her work phone saying how hurt I was that she blew off my birthday. The next day I was out till late afternoon and arrived home with a blinking light on my answering machine. I played the message. It was Gertrude, in a very loud, angry voice yelling at me, saying, "I didn't just 'blow off' your birthday. Sometimes people do forget things. And I think it would be a great idea if you never called me again! GOODBYE!" *Where did all that come from,* I wondered. The next day I tried calling to question what brought all this on and how her perspective had changed. She just hung up when she heard my voice. I attempted to call again a few times over the next few days and left some voice mails trying to determine what went wrong. All I got were hang-ups, or she took her phone off the hook. I didn't understand why I was being shunned again by her.

A year or more passed by when one evening, the phone rang. I said, "Hello?" Then I heard Gertrude's voice blurt out, "My husband is having an affair." He admitted to it. She had left her house to call me. We discussed her situation, and I asked if he knew about me; she said yes. Over the next few months, we talked occasionally as she was still hurting from her husband's infidelity, and I was just trying to be there for her. I knew there was slim to no chance we'd ever get together, but in the back of my mind, I was hoping her husband's affair would be the catalyst for her to get divorced. It never happened. Then, months later when she got over it a bit, she wanted to take me to dinner as a thank you. I said, *"What?"* Now, I did not want to start up another affair with her again and feel all that guilt return. I said, "Does your husband know you want to take me to dinner?" She responded, "Yes." *That's odd,* I thought, *but apparently, he is okay with it.*

We stayed in touch off and on for a few years after that, but we never saw each other again. I still called to chit-chat every now and again. I was a fool not picking up on the signs that she was trying to dump me permanently. When I'd call, she'd say, "I'm sorry; I'm busy," or "Let me call you back." And I believed her. She never called back. I was so naïve about her trying to eliminate me from her life. It wasn't till many years later that a light bulb went off, and I suddenly got it as I replayed the relationship in my head.

The last time I ever talked to her was when I sent her a very nice "Thinking of you" card. Inside the card, I had written a kind note. She did not respond. So, within two days, I called her and asked her if she received it. She said, "Yes, it's in my hand." She seemed odd like something was wrong. It did not come across as positive. A couple of days went by, and in the mail, I received a large white mailing envelope from the insurance company she worked for. It was addressed, in her handwriting, to MR. WILLIAM C. DUCKWORTH. That was odd. She had never addressed an envelope to me like that, using my formal name before. I proceeded to open the envelope, and the only thing inside was the card I had sent her, completely sealed and unopened. I was devastated. I tried to call her, sometimes leaving voice mails. I called several times over the next few weeks but could never get through to her. It was obvious after seventeen years our on-again, off-again relationship was *permanently* over. She blindsided me, and I did not see that coming.

I ended up writing a letter to her asking for closure and just to explain why suddenly, without warning, she had cut me off abruptly from her life and never gave a reason. That was in 2006. She never ever had the decency to respond to me. *SHAME ON YOU GERTRUDE!* I just wanted closure, and I'd understand. But she just left me hanging to this day in limbo as to what were the actual reasons. I don't know exactly what triggered it. I suspect she must have been in marriage counseling, and the counselor told her to cut off all contact with me, even if I'd tried contacting her to just ignore me. If I were the one who decided to cut off contact and make a clean break after *now* knowing her intimately, I would have had the decency to write a compassionate letter explaining why I was permanently breaking it off. I would *not* have left her hanging as she did me. That was cruel, considering how well we knew each other. Had we been casual acquaintances, then I would understand not hearing from her.

She caused me more depression, and for years, I couldn't get her out of my mind. It was hard to believe because she had married her high school sweetheart at eighteen. Both spouses had affairs, but they remained married. I met her when I was around twenty-five, and she ghosted me at age forty-two. It took me ten long years of therapy to get over her to the point where she no longer consumed me, and she stopped being on my mind every hour of the day. She did a real number on me mentally, which does not even begin to scratch the surface of the emotional pain she caused me. My life would have been better off if I had never met her.

My love for music has helped me therapeutically get through rough times; in this case, it was brought on by the ice-cold Gertrude. While trying to recover from a broken heart and get back on my feet, these songs worked as my musical prescription: "I'm Still Standing" by Elton John and "You Give Love a Bad Name" by Bon Jovi.

In the process of writing this chapter, all the great memories have resurfaced, and I must admit I still miss her terribly. Before or since meeting her, I have never met someone I was so compatible with when things were at their peak. The good times were really good. But the bad times when she dumped me sent me into a deep nosedive into the abyss of depression, worse than when my adopted mom died. When she ghosted me, I fell into a heavy drinking binge for years, trying to escape dealing with the deep emotional pain she caused me.

I started this chapter off by stating that the regret I have has positive and negative connotations. I will now explain. The negative regret I have was that I should have never gotten involved with a married woman. I could have avoided the massive guilt I lived with for years that ate me alive inside. She mentally screwed with my mind and led me on with promises she never fulfilled. Had she never come into my life that would have spared me *MY* greatest disappointment and heartache I have ever experienced. The positive regret stems from all the good times I had with Gertrude that I will never experience with her again. Those great memories will be something I will always cherish for the rest of my life. She was a double-edged sword in my life. She was the perfect one for me. The great memories I have of Gertrude torture me in a good way. There were so many positive romantic emotions that took me to the summit of Mount Everest. I've never known anyone else that could make me feel so happy and *wanted*. They are priceless treasured memories that I will always hold dearly close to my heart. Unfortunately, she still crosses my mind daily. She once told me in the nineties that she always wanted to stay in touch with me. It's a funny thing how people can have a change of heart over time.

Lord Alfred Tennyson once wrote, "Tis better to have loved and lost than to never have loved at all." I added to the quote, FALSE! It is better to have never loved at all.

In conclusion, during this painful chapter in my life, Gertrude knew better than to break her vows and string me along for all those years. She unfairly played with my emotions. Had she been single, there would have been a whole different set of ground rules, and I would have never experienced the terrible guilt.

Let me state here and say *YES, I KNEW THIS WAS WRONG*. However, for the very first time in my life, I had someone who legitimately loved me. I went down the wrong road and paid the high price, but I couldn't help myself. With what you have read about my romantic life up to this point, walk a mile in my shoes. If women had always rejected you, and you see that all your friends are married, what would you do? Could your willpower hold *YOU* back? Think about it. At the time she came along, I had never experienced an overwhelming relationship that took me to such a high. It was simply mind-blowing. If you were me, do you really think your willpower could stop you from going down the treacherous road I did? Let it sink in; use your deep thought; honestly, determine if you could have walked away from the temptation I once knew.

The way it felt to be ultimately rejected by her can best be described like this: It felt like she ripped my heart out of my chest and ran it through a shredder!

Gertrude, if you're reading this, I want you to know I would have worshiped you with all my love and spoiled you like a queen. There are no words to describe how terribly you hurt me. I'm in a far better place at this point in my life than when you knew me. I'm living my best years now, and you could have been a part of it. Now, I'm the happiest I have ever been in my lifetime. You're missing out. Oh well, it is your loss!

I have written many poems and lyrics about certain women that had made a major impact on my life. Some of these poems are positive, and some are negative. Having known Gertrude there are plenty of both. I wrote the following lyrics that sum up how truly bad Gertrude broke my heart.

Wicked As a Witch

Oh, when we first met,
You put me on cloud nine.
Oh, when we first met,
You were sweet as wine.

Oh, you stole my heart.
You made me feel like number one.
Oh, you stole my heart.
Now we're over and done.

Oh, you told me
That you loved me so much.
Oh, you told me
You shiver upon my touch.

You dumped me!
You're as wicked as a Witch!
You drove a knife through my heart!
You're as wicked as a Witch!

You screwed me!
You're as wicked as a Witch!
You really, really hurt me!
You're as wicked as a Witch!

Oh, you used to be so sweet.
Then you told lies to me.
Oh, you used to be so sweet.
Never meant to be were we?

Oh, you led me on.
And I fell for you like a fool.
Oh, you led me on.

You B***H! You are so cruel!

Oh, you were so sly.
You fooled me from the start.
Oh, you were so sly.
You tore my heart apart.

You dump me!
You're as wicked as a Witch!
You drove a knife through my heart!
You're as wicked as a Witch!

You screwed me!
You're as wicked as a Witch!
You really, really hurt me!
You're as wicked as a Witch!

AND WITCHES ALWAYS BURN….

— WILLIAM COWELL DUCKWORTH
September 9, 2017

Side notes: For inspiration, I used the "Wicked Witch of the West" from *The Wizard of Oz*. When things were good, I had selected "Wicked Game" by Chris Isaak as our song.

Chapter 15

Detour

Until now, you have been reading about how my life has unfolded. In this chapter, I'd like to veer off this course and take you on a *detour* so you can get to know a bit more about who *I* am, my interests, and some important highlights that stand out to me in my life.

For the majority of my life, I've spent it as a metaphorical nomad. I have been drifting through my life trying to figure out what I'm doing here and what my purpose is on this planet. I'm a lost soul, so to speak with lack of direction. I've suffered deep depression much of my life. I've tried to figure out where I fit in. Until recently, I hadn't found myself and had been searching for answers. It's troubling to go through life without answers or a purpose, trying to find my way. For some people, it seems everything has fallen into place, and things, in general, are unfolding as they should. Most people have found a spouse whom they love, at least half have before the divorce rate kicks in, laughing out loud (LOL), had their children, and have a decent job (they may not like but it pays enough in most cases to be successful). They work till they retire and then enjoy their golden years before they pass away.

My life never followed that path as an adult. I remember when I was in college, I *assumed* that once I graduated, I would get a good corporate job, company car included, and climb the corporate ladder, find a spouse, and be happily married for the rest of my life before retiring as an executive.

Ever since I was eight years old, there has been a large part of me that has always wanted to be famous for something that I've accomplished, such as an actor, rock star, politician, NFL player, race car driver, writer/author, or even an astronaut.

In high school, that first opportunity to attempt my dream of being famous arose when I met my musical writing partner, Charles Brown, and we formed the band Stonehenge. I write the lyrics, and Charles writes the music. We have been a writing team since ninth grade, and it still continues forty-nine years later. Charles introduced me to The Who in 1974 when I was fifteen. I had never heard of them before and quickly became enamored. Ever since then, I have become an addict of The Who. I have a T-shirt that reads, "Music is my drug, and The Who are my dealer." I simply call myself a *Who-a-holic*.

Well, we were going to be the next The Who. We were focused on becoming successful rock stars. Now, don't laugh, but if I could have chosen any profession and knew that I would be successful at it, I'd *still*, to this day, want to become a rock star along with the likes of Roger Daltrey, Billy Joel, and John Mellencamp, to mention a few. That dream never came to fruition.

I have attempted several times to learn piano and guitar but lack the discipline to practice as it seems more of a chore and took the fun out of learning to play an instrument. It's sad, really, because I have melodies in my head that would complement the lyrics I write. I think I could be a good songwriter if I just knew how to play. I've learned over the course of my life that I'm better suited at writing the written word. Maybe it was for the best that I never became a rock star because after reading through rock stars' biographies, most of them got screwed over by signing bad contracts.

Having grown up with a mother who was always involved in politics, it rubbed off on me. For a long time, up until the 2000s, I had a desire to be a politician. I thought I could do a better job than most of those politicians in Washington, D.C., or at the state level. One thing is for certain: I could never have been bought to vote a certain way. I would have always voted my conscience and forgotten about the backroom deals. When I was heading down that road, I worked on many campaigns, interacted with politicians on the state level, and completed an internship for a United States Senator from Colorado. I learned politics is a *who you know* and not *what you know* profession. Given today's political climate, there is not enough money in the world to get me to go back into politics.

In the 1990s, at one point in time in my late twenties or early thirties, I attempted to be a model. This was spurred on by relatives and others who encouraged me to investigate it. I was still styling the GQ look back then and was much thinner in those days. I had professional photos taken. I met with a famous modeling agency in Denver, and they said if I moved to New York City, I should not have a problem making it. That move was not on my agenda, but I was up for doing local work.

Nothing became of that except it led to me being cast in a film as a paid extra that was being shot in Denver. I have a love for films and was elated to have dabbled in the making of two films in Denver, Colorado. That film was called *3 Ninjas High Noon at Mega Mountain*. It's what I would call a children's movie, and in my opinion, it was geared to an audience from ages four to fourteen. It was one of the installments in a series of the *3 Ninjas* films. It starred Loni Anderson, Hulk Hogan, and the late Jim Varney. I was in three scenes but only showed up in one for a semi-close-up where I'm on screen for a whopping three seconds. This movie took place at an amusement park in Denver that was called Elitch Gardens at the time, which doubled as Mega Mountain.

Loni Anderson was dressed as a Dominatrix and played an evil character who commandeers and closes the amusement park and uses the patrons as trapped hostages. Loni's character demands a ransom before she will open the park and let all the hostages go. It just so happens that the *3 Ninja* kids, who range from grade school to high school freshman age, just happen to be at Mega Mountain as patrons that day. They came to the rescue with their martial arts skills and saved the day. In my opinion, the movie was terrible and only stayed in the theaters in Denver for about two weeks. I bought a VHS copy of the film. This was long before DVDs hit the scene.

The other film I worked on as a production assistant in Denver was not a bad one but went straight to the internet and did not even make it to DVD, as far as I'm aware. The name of this film is *Assassins' Code* which starred Martin Kove, who played John Kreese in *The Karate Kid* (the mean karate teacher). I had the opportunity to meet and chat with Mr. Kove briefly a few times during the filming of the movie. Mr. Kove was an extremely nice guy, but let me tell you, he was just as intimidating in real life as he was in *The Karate Kid*. I was lucky enough to get his autograph. He wrote, "To Bill, great working with ya! But remember No Mercy Marty 'Sensei' Kove." The late Richard Moll, who also worked on the film, played "Bull" on Night Court. I was able to get his autograph as well, and he signed it "Bill- See you in court! Richard Moll 'Bull'." John Savage, of *Apocalypse Now* fame, and Christopher Atkins, whom you may remember from *The Blue Lagoon* with Brooke Shields, were in the film as well, whom I both met on set. I wanted to ask Christopher Atkins, as a joke, if he could give me Brook Shields's number. Of course, I never did. Not only did I work as a production assistant, but I had an impromptu appearance in that movie as well.

During filming one day, on the fly, it was decided they needed a janitor/maintenance man character. They came to me to play that guy. They dressed me up with a tool belt. My few seconds on screen were to scrape off letters of the character's name on an office window who had been fired in the film. We did around four takes because I was nervous. When I saw the film online, only my arm showed up, scraping off the letters, which I kept as a souvenir. *Assassins' Code* was an espionage film about a disc that was wanted. That was the end of my film career of long hours. I only got paid $40 for my work on the *3 Ninjas* for two days of work. I think that was scale for an extra, $20 a day.

Before I knew of the production assistant job for *Assassins' Code,* I had been volunteering for three months at the Colorado Film Commission. I dressed in business attire with an open collar and no tie. I was hoping if I dressed professionally and showed up faithfully, it would show my dedication. I was hoping to land a paid position with them. Unfortunately, I was not hired. But my experience with the Colorado Film Commission led to my work on *Assassins' Code*.

Music plays an important part in my life. Basically, I'm a classic rock guy, but I do like other genres as well: rockabilly, symphonies, reggae, a little folk, limited country, and a few others. I will even travel to see the right band. I love to collect rock 'n' roll memorabilia. The decor theme of my home is hard rock and resembles a internationally known café (a work that is forever in progress).

The most prized possession of my collectible classic rock memorabilia is an autographed microphone signed by Roger Daltrey that he used on

The Who's 50th-anniversary tour at a concert in Milan, Italy. I won the bid for that through The Who online auction fundraiser for Teen Cancer America (TCA). TCA is a foundation Roger Daltrey put together for kids with cancer. It provides a ward in the hospital for these kids to be with other kids with cancer in their teenage years. They can play ping pong, listen to music, and socialize with their own peers. This way, they don't have to be stuck in bed in a hospital room with adult patients.

One evening while I was living in Denver, I went to see the late Dick Dale, king of the surf guitar, in a dive bar. After the show, while walking out of the bar, they had a list of upcoming bands, some well-known names, but mainly local bands from the Denver area. I stopped to take a look at the list and noticed there was a tribute band to The Who coming called The Substitutes, named after one of The Who songs. I thought, *Wow! I've got to see these guys!* When the night finally came, I was expecting a half-assed band version of The Who songs. Boy, was I wrong. The Substitutes were absolutely fantastic! I was blown away by how good these guys were, and they are a Denver-based band! They were so good, in fact, I knew I had to befriend them. I saw them a few more times, and each time, I personally thanked each member for a job well done.

As I was getting to know them, I started hanging out with them before and after the shows. Sometimes, I have even become a part-time roadie, helping them load in and load out at different gigs. I was so impressed with them that to my own volition, I took it upon myself to volunteer to help promote The Substitutes, mostly at my own expense. The first thing I did was take their business card and spruce it up. It includes their website and Facebook page information. The next thing I did was to get t-shirts made up to sell at the shows. The leader of the band, drummer Pete Ward, trusted me to design the back of the t-shirts. (We had both contributed to the cost of having the shirts made up.) I explained that I wanted to put the name of the band on the back, along with their website and Facebook address information. He let me add the phrase "WHERE THERE IS NO SUBSTITUTE THERE IS ONLY …the substitutes" and choose the font and color of the lettering. The Who colors, of course, match the Union Jack flag. Then I got a tip jar, dressed up with their name and logo placed on the front. It looked like a decal from a distance. I initiated a sign-up sheet to recruit fans at shows so The Substitutes fans could keep up with the ongoing status of the band's happenings.

I also worked the crowd during the shows. When I saw people grooving to The Substitutes during the shows, I would hand them a Substitutes' business card along with the Substitutes' campaign-style button I had designed. I worked intently, trying to build up their fan base. Pete Ward will no doubt confirm that I am The Substitutes' number-one fan, and I've become an honorary member of the band, like the fifth Beatle, so to speak. I even recommended my musical writing partner, Charles, to fill in the acoustic guitar parts where needed on specific songs. Charles got the job. I had been with The Substitutes at every show except for one over the four or five years I was able to follow them before I moved out of Denver. At the last live show before I made the move to Myrtle Beach, they floored me and caught me off guard. In the middle of the show, they announced to the audience that I was moving away, and they had worked on a song they dedicated to me. It was off *Live at Leeds,* and my memory of the song is a bit foggy, but I think it was "Young Man Blues." Thank you, my Dear Boys! You know who you are.

I have many interests: photography, movies, traveling, auto racing, writing, history, reading, the beach, and collecting rock and roll memorabilia. I'm an automobile enthusiast and a wannabe surfer. Speaking of auto racing, I really enjoyed having the opportunity to attend a racecar driving school back in the nineties in Denver. It was a two-day course learning to drive and race Spec racers. I had a blast! I felt like Tom Cruise, as it was around the time *Days of Thunder* was in theaters.

Currently, I have developed a love for writing books. I hope to write more, as I have two others I'm currently working on, one of which will be my next book on OCD and what it's like living with it firsthand. In addition, I still have a passion for writing my poems and lyrics. I attempted to write my first song while I was in junior high school. In my junior high school years, I wrote six songs on the piano. I've written 128 lyrics for songs and forty-five poems to date and have countless unfinished works of stanzas, single lines, and ideas for potential lyrics, poems, and books.

As mentioned, I really love writing. The paper is my canvas, and the pen is my paintbrush. It is there that I can dig down deep inside and express my inner emotions. No one knows what I'm feeling until they see my written words. Some of my poetry is dark and sad as I have reflected on my inner personal school of life experiences. On the other hand, some of my poetry is upbeat, and I have written some of the most romantic poems about women I have had feelings for.

So, there you have it. You've gotten to know somewhat of who I am. My adoptive dad never took the time to learn what I was all about—his loss.

Chapter 16

The Premonition

In 1997, I felt a strong, uncomfortable feeling that my adoptive mom was going to die. I have no idea what brought this on. She was not ill and was in good health. I am not a religious man, but I had a premonition even though I do not believe in that sort of thing. So, I felt I needed to get things right with my mom before something happened to her. I told her I'd miss her when she was gone and wasn't sure how I was going to deal with that. She said, "I will always be with you if you want me to be." That felt comforting.

I started telling her how much Dad had hurt me over the years. She knew and was a witness to a lot of it. She knew what a *bastard* he could be. She added, "Your father should never have had children." I must second that statement. My father could not relate well with other people. Dad thought about himself and put his concerns first rather than the people he hurt who were close to him in terms of relatives and ex-wives.

I had indicated to my mom that I thought she would die within two years. She was between the ages of sixty-eight and sixty-nine. I was trying to figure out what her life span would be based on the ages of her parents when they died. Her father died at age seventy-seven, and her mother died at age seventy-eight. I think this spurred on the strange feeling of sureness that I had almost felt something inside that positively would make it so.

About a year and a half went by without incident. During that time, my mom and her boyfriend, who was a few years older than she was, were in the process of planning a trip to Egypt to see the pyramids with a tour group. It sounded like a once-in-a-lifetime trip, and I had always wanted to see the pyramids myself. I asked my mom if I could go with them.

Mom answered with a very swift and firm "NO!" *Ok, Jeez,* I thought. *I guess they don't want me around on this trip.* Oh, but to find out later my mom's boyfriend's son and his girlfriend were invited along, I wondered, *What's up with that?*

My mom could be selfish and extremely inconsiderate of my time often. She had always insisted, no demanded says it better, that when they traveled together, I was their damn chauffeur, and if I tried to balk at it, that would not fly with Mom. So, inconsiderate by not asking politely if I would be able to take them to the airport, she would say it like this, "I want you to take us to the airport on such and such date." I will never forget a previous trip when Mom and her boyfriend flew to a convention in New Orleans related to her boyfriend's work. It was an early morning flight. At the time, I was working a part-time job at a local video store to keep some money coming in, and on my days off, I would be job searching for a more career-type of employment. I worked the night shifts at the video store, which meant I did not get off work till 1 a.m. I got little sleep that night as I had to get up around 5 a.m., having only got four hours of sleep and playing chauffeur. Mom could *care less* that I was only getting four hours of sleep because she was using me as her personal taxi to be at her beck and call at the drop of a hat. If she had asked me once, that would be one thing, but she just assumed I was her taxi service. Her boyfriend had two children who lived in the Denver area, but they never took them to the airport, as I recall. After picking up her boyfriend and heading to Denver International Airport (DIA), which was about a forty-fifty-minute drive because DIA is located far to the east of Denver on the plains. DIA is located twenty-five miles from Downtown Denver.

October 30, 1999, was the day when I was enlisted again to take her and her boyfriend to DIA early in the morning. When we arrived at the airport around 6 a.m., I helped them unload the luggage from my car. As they went through the sliding glass doors of the terminal, I saw my mother for the very last time. As she disappeared out of sight right then, a sudden thought went through my mind. *Maybe that's the last time I will see her.* It felt like a very weird thought. I just blew off that thought for a while. Later in the afternoon, back at my place, around 3 p.m., I was heading down the stairs to my family room. While moving down the staircase, another weird thought went through my mind for a second time as I was pondering where they were on their long journey to Egypt. *Maybe their plane will crash. Ah, that never happens.*

Later that evening, I went to see the new Meryl Streep film *Music of the Heart*. I had just arrived home around 9:30 p.m. when the phone rang. It was my mom. I asked her where she was enroute on her trip. She replied, "We're still in the New York Airport and still waiting for the flight. It's got a mechanical problem, and we're waiting for it to arrive from Los Angeles. So, we've just been sitting around drinking, and I thought I'd give you a call." *Wow,* I thought. I had figured they might well be across the Atlantic Ocean by now, possibly only a few hours out from landing in Egypt. The conversation did not last long.

Early the next morning, on October 31, 1999, I was awakened by a ringing telephone around five or six in the morning. It was my mom's current cleaning lady saying, "I think your mom's plane crashed."

"What?" I asked, surprisingly. I turned on the TV by my bed with the remote. I saw the "Breaking News" coming from the television. Then I told her I needed to go check on something, and I'd be right back. I jumped out of bed and ran to the kitchen to grab her itinerary to verify the flight number. Sure enough, the flight number matched. It truly was EgyptAir Flight 990. I then told my mom's cleaning lady that I had to go and hung up. For some reason, my first reaction was to call my friend Tim, who's known my mom since we were in ninth grade. I have always felt the need to tell people what's going on in my life when I should be more private. I am much too open with people. As Tim answered the phone, I blurted out in a loud voice, "My mom's plane just crashed; it's on the news. I gotta go," and hung up. I was shocked but not extremely shocked because in the back of my mind, I had been expecting this. It was not as big of a surprise as you might think. My Aunt Mary, the youngest of my mom's two sisters, lived about two blocks away in the same townhome community I lived in. I needed to rush over there ASAP to let her know. However, before I could even think about going over, my OCD had such control over my life that I needed to jump in the shower to feel clean; otherwise, I would feel too much anxiety that I was dirty and couldn't focus on the matter at hand. It was my standard thirty-minute shower, and I couldn't rush it or skimp. Even in an emergency, that darn OCD takes precedence. I then drove to my aunt's place. Once I arrived, I went through her back gate, which opened to a small back patio, and I marched right up to her sliding glass door and knocked on the glass. She had her telephone up to her ear as she opened the sliding glass door.

The television on her kitchen counter was on with live coverage of the crash. She was on hold and told me she was on the emergency line that could tell you the names of which passengers were on that flight. I said, "If you already knew the plane had crashed, why didn't you call me first?"

Mary replied, "I was going to call you as soon as I could verify if they were on the flight or not."

That kinda pissed me off as this was important and felt she should have notified me there was a crash before she determined who was on that flight.

Meanwhile, the breaking news on the television was showing the large debris field of broken, fragmented sections of the plane along with luggage, clothes, and possibly some human remains spewed all over the place along with floating jet fuel. "By the time rescue ships and helicopters arrived, it was obvious that there would be no survivors" (Langewiesche). The plane crashed nearly sixty miles south of Nantucket Island, Massachusetts, into the Atlantic Ocean. All 217 passengers and crew perished. My aunt was still on the phone to verify that my mother and her boyfriend and his son and girlfriend were aboard. We finally did get confirmation.

Just as my gut predicted, my mom died within that two-year window. It was mind-blowing bizarre how that came true. Now that's three out of four parents that I have had who have been *killed* and not die of natural causes. My mom was seventy.

Chapter 17

Dealing with Another Tragedy/ Coping with Awkward Family Matters

It was Halloween morning, and life just threw me another curveball. This was not what I had planned for my day ahead. How was I going to handle this? A set of unforeseen circumstances forced me to go down this rough road and find out where it would lead me. It was a weird day, obviously. Originally, my plans were to go over to my mom's house at night and hand out all the candy to the trick-or-treaters. The EgyptAir crash changed all that.

As the day progressed, my cousin Kim (Mary's daughter), Mom's other sister, and her daughter all gathered at my aunt Mary's home. I was not in the mood to take any calls. I just wanted to hang out with family. I was kind of in a daze. Kim had cleverly set up my mom's telephone number to ring at my aunt's place. I had given instructions that I was *not* taking any calls but to at least let me know who was calling on the off chance it was someone I wanted to talk to.

Back when I had the gut premonition that my (adoptive) mom would die in two years, I already had determined if the press or local television news station ever contacted me and wanted to shove a microphone and camera in my face and ask, "How do you feel now that your mom was killed aboard EgyptAir Flight 990?" the first thing I would *want* to say is, "How the F**K do you think I feel? My mom was just killed!" I was going to deny the joy of the news organization that victory. I always hate how local TV news stations or national press track down family members in a tragic situation to get a comment to scoop their competition. Getting the story for the evening news can be so intrusive and inconsiderate. If it bleeds, it leads.

Sure enough, one of the local TV news stations had called my mom's number, and the phone rang at my aunt's home. My cousin Kim answered. They wanted to talk to me. I refused to take their call. As mentioned previously, I was not going to talk to them during such a difficult time for ratings, so they could get the scoop over their competitors. I was not in the right frame of mind to talk with them anyway. Ironically, the local press reached out to my mom's boyfriend's children, and they chose to speak on camera to the press. I saw them on the local news that night and was surprised they had agreed to it.

That night, I returned to my residence, drank a few beers, and started to process the hell of a day I'd just been through. The next morning, I was back at my aunt's place, and service arrangements for my mom began. Suggestions were being made, but it was my call to give final approval.

My mom had worked as a clerk at the Colorado State Capitol in the House of Representatives since 1978. Each clerk was assigned to one row, assisting Republicans and Democrats on each side of the aisle with their needs. Over the years, by the time my mom was killed, she had worked her way up through the ranks to become the House's Chief Assignable Clerk.

For the memorial service, one of my mother's best friends worked at the Capitol and was able to make the Colorado State Supreme Court chambers in the Capitol building available. That was a perfect location, as my mom always loved the State Capitol Building. She would refer to it affectionately as "The Golden Dome." This was because the Colorado State Capitol dome is covered in gold leaf, making the building a beautiful sight.

Meanwhile, I was in touch with my sister, who had been living in Marrakesh, Morocco, for the last six years. I really wanted her to come to Mom's service even though Mom and she didn't get along. I thought it was important for her to be there. She arrived on the eve of the service. I picked her up from the airport and arrived at my mom's cousin's home, where all of my mom's relatives, who were able to attend, gathered for dinner. There was catching up to do as we all had not seen each other for some time. However, underneath the brave faces we were putting on and attempting cheer, we all knew we were there for a somber reason. Even my aunt Allison flew in for the service.

On the day of the service, I was too broken up to say anything and remained seated. Over the years, my mother had made many political contacts. The first person to speak was the Honorable United States Congressman Scott McInnis, who represented one of the districts in Colorado. He had known Mom from when he was a Colorado State Representative while Mom was working as a clerk. I had no idea he would be there, but I was very impressed. He gave a thoughtful speech about Mom and then walked over and handed me a plaque with the front page of *The Congressional Record* (framed) dated Wednesday, November 3, 1999. *The Congressional Record* is a big deal. I remember when I interned in Washington, DC, *The Congressional Record* was printed daily and published what business had transpired on Capitol Hill by both Houses the day before. On Capitol Hill, it was free and readily available to anyone who wanted an issue. I remember thinking, *God, I wish Mom were alive to tell her SHE MADE* THE CONGRESSIONAL RECORD! I was appreciative that the Congressman took the time to write about Mom in *The Congressional Record* and have people she never knew read about her.

After the Congressman spoke, several other people, such as her friends and coworkers, praised Mom for how nice she was. I found it a bit odd because I had, for the most part, a negative relationship with her. I had to grow up in her household.

Mom was a control freak and liked to always be in charge. I did not see the wonderfulness everyone else saw. Mom and I would argue quite often, and I believe it was due to her constant demands, wanting it done *now!* Not five minutes from now! Otherwise, she would become angry with me. Mom also laid some major guilt trips on me, making me feel like a heel and a bad person. When I shared the guilt trips of what Mom said with others, they were surprised Mom said those things to me. Heck, I can honestly say that I don't fully feel like she loved me 100% based on some of her actions over the time I knew her.

That night, back at my townhome, my sister and I got into a really big argument over some private family matters. It also stemmed from my point of view that I was under the impression my sister came for Mom's service. My sister then informed me that she came to support me. And she made the comment something to the effect that "You seem to have it all together and don't seem to be that upset." That was true, but it was because, psychologically, I had been mentally preparing for this day.

Our argument had gotten heated, and there was a lot of disagreement. Over the next few days, the relationship between my sister and me became extremely strained, very close to the point that we might never have spoken to each other again in our lives. Personally, for me, it really stressed me out. Only a few other relatives that I had spoken with regarding the issues my sister and I were having picked up on the fact that there was extreme tension between my sister and me. A few days after the service, a few of my relatives, including my aunt, who was my biological father's sister, my sister, and my mother's two sisters, and I met for dinner at her hotel. Once we were all seated at the table, my aunt from back East was blunt and said something to the effect, "We need to address the elephant in the room," and told my sister and I we needed to resolve this. I remember I asked to speak with my sister in private. We left the table, and after trying to resolve the issue, it turned out to be futile. More days went by, and my sister and I were not speaking. Then my sister called me and said she wanted to remain in contact, and she didn't want to lose me as a brother over this conflict where we would never speak again. I was open to the idea, but our positions did not change. We stayed in touch, and eventually, many years later, we got the issues resolved to acceptable terms between us.

For the first three months after my mother was killed, in the back of my mind, I held out hope that my mom would be able to make it to a phone and call me and say, "I made it. I'm ok." But I knew better.

One of the things that helped me deal with my mom's death was to listen to "Let It Be" by the Beatles. In that song, Paul McCartney keeps repeating "Let it Be, Let it Be." That song helped me because *I* just had to *let it be.* I could not reverse time or the outcome of the fate that happened. So, as the song says, I just had to accept reality, put it to rest, just "Let it Be," and move forward as best I could.

I had a dream about my adoptive mom approximately six months after she was killed. It was a strange type of dream I'd never experienced before in my life. I had dreamt my mom and I were standing in her kitchen the night before the flight. I had the itinerary in front of me, and I said to her, "Mom, you can't go on that flight because the plane is going to crash." She looked at me very seriously and said in a matter-of-fact way, "No, I have to go." It was so strange. It was as if she knew it were her time and *needed* to be on that flight. I was a little freaked out when I woke up and remembered that dream. It had seemed surreal.

Chapter 18

Cause of the Crash of EgyptAir Flight 990 and Greed

On the evening of October 30, 1999, EgyptAir Flight 990 departed Los Angeles International Airport bound for Cairo with a scheduled stopover at New York City's JFK Airport. The 767-airliner touched down at JFK at approximately 11:48 p.m. Eastern Standard Time. Aboard were a total of 217 passengers (crew included) when the plane left the gate for Cairo. The passenger manifest consisted of nationalities from seven countries: United States, Egypt (including thirty-three Egyptian military officers among other Egyptians aboard), Canada, Syria, Germany, Sudan, and Zimbabwe. Out of the 217 passengers, 54 of them, many elderly, were with the tour group my mom was with.

At approximately 1:20 a.m., the plane lifted off for its ten-hour flight to Cairo. The cockpit crew consisted of Captain Ahmed El-Habashi, 57; First Officer Adel Anwar, 36; relief Captain Raouf Noureldin, 52; relief First Officer Gameel AL-Batouti, 59; and chief pilot Captain Hatem Rushdy.

> …the flight required two complete flight crews, each consisting of one captain and one first officer. EgyptAir designated one crew as the "active crew" and the other as the "cruise crew," sometimes also referred to as the "relief crew." While no formal procedure was specified when each crew flew the aircraft, the active crew customarily made the takeoff and flew the first four to five hours of the flight. The cruise crew then assumed control of the aircraft until about one to two hours before landing, when the active crew returned to the cockpit and assumed control of the aircraft. EgyptAir designated the captain of the active crew as the pilot-in-command or the commander of the flight ("Cockpit Crew").

Twenty minutes into the flight at 1:40 a.m., as the plane was in the process of climbing to its assigned altitude, the Cockpit Voice Recorder (CVR) revealed that the relief first officer, Al-Batouti, arrived in the cockpit and suggested that he relieve the Command first officer who was at the controls. Al-Batouti wasn't sleepy and would remain awake, so why doesn't he start flying his portion of the flight now. A bit of an argument ensued. The command first officer indicated that he had gotten plenty of sleep and was not tired. Al-Batouti then said, "You mean you are not going to get up? You will get up, go and get some rest and come back" (NTSB 3). After conversing back and forth and the two men disagreeing with each other. Al-Batouti indicated he would go eat and come back. The first command officer suggested Al-Batouti just bring his meal back to the cockpit, and then they would switch out seats, and the command first officer would then agree to go to sleep (NTSB 3).

A few minutes later, the CVR heard the cockpit door opening, indicating Al-Batouti returned with his meal. Then the sound of an electric seat conversation was picked up, and it indicated that the relief first officer moved into the command first officer's seat. The Flight Data Recorder (FDR) and radar information indicated that the plane had reached its assigned altitude and leveled off.

At 1:48:03, the command captain excused himself to use the bathroom. At approximately 1:48:40, "the relief first officer stated quietly, 'I rely on God'" (NTSB 4). The flight recorders did not pick up sounds or events that would indicate any unusual circumstances to indicate that anything was going wrong that would precede him saying, "I rely on God."

At 1:49:45, the FDR indicated that the autopilot was disconnected. Then the left elevator made a slight change to a nose-up deflection, and the right elevator also made a slight change to a nose-down deflection, but the plane basically remained flying level. At 1:49:48, the first relief officer stated once again, "I rely on God." (NTSB 4). "At 1:49:53, the throttle levers were moved from their cruise power setting to idle, and at 1:49:54, the FDR recorded an abrupt nose-down elevator movement and a very slight movement of the inboard ailerons. Subsequently, the airplane began to rapidly pitch nose down and descend" (NTSB 4).

At 1:49:57 to 1:50:05, the first relief pilot repeated seven more times, "I rely on God" (NTSB 5). At the same time, the "...result of the nose-down elevator position the planes load factor decreased approximately from 1 to around 0.2 G" (NTSB 5). Approximately 11 seconds later, due to the movement of elevators in a nose-down position, the "FDR recorded additional, slightly larger inboard aileron movements, and the elevators started further in the nose-down direction" (NTSB 5).

By this time, the captain had made it back to the cockpit. The CVR reveals at 1:50:06 the captain asking loudly, "What's happening? What's happening" (NTSB 5)?

By this time, the load factor of the aircraft was decreasing further as the increased deflection from the nose-down elevator was now "reaching negative G..." (NTSB 5).

Then, once again, for the tenth time at 1:50:07, the relief first officer repeated, "I rely on God" (NTSB 5). At the same time, "the CVR recorded sounds of numerous thumps and clips, which continued for about 15 seconds" (NTSB 5). "Habashi [the command captain] was clearly pulling very hard on his control yoke, trying desperately to raise the nose. Even so, thirty seconds into the dive, at 22,000 feet, the airplane hit the speed of sound....Batouti [the relief first officer] reached over and shut off the fuel, killing the engines....The speed-brake handle was then pulled, deploying drag devices on the wings" (Langewiesche).

"At the same time, there was an unusual occurrence back at the tail: the right-side and left-side elevators, which normally move together to control the airplane's pitch, began to 'split,' or move in opposite directions. Specifically: the elevator on the right remained down, while the left side elevator moved up to a healthy recovery position.... but the essence in this case, seemed to be that Batouti was pushing down the right elevator while the captain was pulling up the left elevator" (Langewiesche).

Because "the engines had been cut, all nonessential electrical devices were lost" (Langewiesche). This cut off the recording of the black boxes, and most of the instrument panels, along with lighting, left the pilots in darkness. "Radar reconstruction showed that the 767 recovered from the dive at 16,000 feet and, like a great wounded glider soared steeply back to 24,000 feet, turned to the southeast while beginning to break apart, and shed its useless left engine and some of its skin before giving up for good and diving to its death at high speed" (Langewiesche). The time of the crash was estimated to be 1:52 am Eastern Standard Time.

The probable cause by the NTSB for this airliner crash after a full investigation concluded in their "Aircraft Accident Brief" below is the result of their findings:

> The National Transportation Safety Board determines that the probable cause of the EgyptAir flight 990 accident is the airplane's departure from normal cruise flight and subsequent impact with the Atlantic Ocean as a result of the relief first officer's flight control inputs. The reason for the relief first officer's actions was not determined. (NTSB 67)

The Egyptians rejected the results from the NTSB report. According to the article in the *Atlantic Monthly,* November 2001, written by William Langewiesche "THE CRASH OF EGYPTAIR 990," states that NTSB showed a lack of concern for cultural sensitivity with what was recorded on the CVR. They took the point of view that when Batouti said, "Tawakkalt ala Allah," (I rely on God), he was not preparing himself to die but on the contrary. They say he was responding to a sudden surprise that something went wrong, and he took evasive action to counteract a missile or another plane, and that's why he started into a dive, and if that was not the case, then the airplane dove on its own.

EgyptAir also claimed, "In its August 11, 2000, submission, EgyptAir asserted that ground tests and simulations conducted during the investigation were flawed because simulations were conducted using Boeings published 767 data and 'did not reflect the actual operation of the airplane'" (NTSB 47). EgyptAir also, in their submission, claimed "…that the relief first officer did not deliberately cause the accident" (NTSB 47).

In short, the Egyptian Civil Aviation Agency (ECAA) rejected the findings of the NTSB. They had concluded a completely different scenario for how the accident occurred. They accused the NTSB of making a rush-to-judgment decision and not taking in all the facts. The ECAA did not believe the NTSB investigation was objective or unbiased and did not feel they did a professional investigation.

Suspective Motive

According to the *Atlantic Monthly* article of November 2001, the Federal Bureau of Investigation (FBI) started a criminal investigation on Batouti for any evidence of why he may have intentionally crashed the plane. Batouti, had flown many international fights back and forth from Egypt to the United States. EgyptAir crew stayed at the Pennsylvania Hotel in New York City. The FBI had conducted interviews with staff at the Pennsylvania Hotel and "…found that Batouti had a reputation for sexual impropriety—and not merely by the prudish standards of America. It was reported that on multiple occasions over the previous two years, he had been suspected of exposing himself to teenage girls, masturbating in public, following female guests to their rooms, and listening at their doors. Some of the maids, it was said, were afraid of him, and the hotel security guards had once brought him in for questioning and a warning. Apparently, the hotel considered banning him. The FBI learned that EgyptAir was aware of these problems and had warned Batouti to control his behavior" (Langewiesche pp.48-9). Soon, a story surfaced between Batouti and the chief pilot who was also staying at the hotel. It was alleged that they had a possible argument, and the chief pilot theoretically may have taken disciplinary action against Batouti once they arrived back in Cairo. According to the *Atlantic Monthly* 2001 article, this would bring public humiliation upon Batouti. Could that be the motive? Wanting to take revenge in a preemptive strike against his boss? And as collateral damage, the rest of the 216 passengers were innocent victims where fate was beyond their control.

In February of 2000, another EgyptAir pilot who had just landed in London, England, came forward. He was requesting political asylum and claimed he had information on the EgyptAir crash. The FBI and NTSB quickly flew to England to interview him. They were hoping for answers to find out exactly why the plane went down. After interviewing him, they determined he was not credible.

"…when the story of Batouti's sexual improprieties was leaked, further angering the Egyptians. They countered, eventually producing a Boeing 777 captain named Mohamed Badrawi, who had been with the other pilots in New York on a fateful night, testified at length that they were like a band of brothers—that Batouti and the chief pilot got along well and had had no direct confrontations. Rather, Badrawi said, he had acted at times as a 'mediator' between the two men, cautioning Batouti on behalf of the chief pilot to 'grow up' in order to avoid legal problems in the United States" (Langewiesche 49).

Relatives Of Passengers/NTSB Investigation
After the crash and the coming weeks went by, when every family was learning how to cope in their own way, the NTSB kept us updated on how the investigation was going. One of the first things they did was to send out DNA kits to the relative's families; they were to be mailed back so if they found human remains, they could match up to which relatives they were related to. Of course, the fact that I was adopted, I did not need to do this. However, my mother's two sisters did. The NTSB never got back to us, so I assume they never recovered my mom's remains.

The NTSB was fabulous and did not keep us in the dark during the ongoing investigation over the coming year. They did not give us hard-core information, as I'm sure they needed to hold it back for their final report, but as I remember, we felt satisfied that we were kept in the loop.

The NTSB kept in touch with all the relatives, at least in the United States, by conducting telephone conferences in a party-line fashion. We were provided ahead of time of when they were going to be held, and I believe (my memory is a bit foggy with all the exact details as this was during the year 2000). To my best recollection, NTSB chairman Jim Hall was conducting the telephone updates. Although he probably introduced himself over the phone line, however, I don't remember that. But I remember recognizing his voice from watching him on television over the years on other high-profile air disasters.

When the final investigation was over, the NTSB provided, free of charge, each relative who wanted a copy of the official NTSB report and their findings to the best of their ability what caused the crash. The report contained a history of the flight, the complete CVR transcribed, and details of how they investigated the crash, including graphs, charts, the response from the ECAA, and how they dealt with their objections. It is a very detailed report, well over one hundred pages.

One year later, on October 31, 2000, I believe by now, it was fairly well accepted that the relief first officer downed the plane intentionally. However, the Egyptian government held their position that it was some other reason that caused the crash and not pilot suicide. Nevertheless, EgyptAir paid for the relatives to attend a memorial service where a monument was placed dedicated to the tragedy of the people on EgyptAir flight 990 at Brenton Point State Park just outside of Newport, Rhode Island.

EgyptAir Obelisk memorial at Brenton State Park, Rhode Island

There were more than 500 relatives who attended the memorial service. There were huge white tents set up, and lunch was provided. They also had speeches from three different nationalities.

The monument that was erected was very apropos. It was constructed from a large piece of tall granite that is close to seven feet tall. Etched in gold was a dedication to those who lost their lives on October 31, 1999, aboard flight EgyptAir 990. It was repeated on the stone three-four times in different languages that represent who was aboard the fight on that fateful night.

In addition, at the base of the granite monument were bricks that were placed permanently, with each brick containing the name of each of the 217 people who were on that flight. My mother's boyfriend's daughter was on the committee that helped design the memorial. She made sure that four of the bricks, each with the names of her father, my mother, my mother's boyfriend's son, and his girlfriend's names, were all lined up together in a single file.

Back in the town of Newport, Rhode Island, in the local cemetery, another smaller ceremony took place after the dedication at Brenton Point State Park. A burial plot was complete with an open casket filled with flowers, mementos, and items that belonged to people found at the crash site. There was also a very large black headstone placed at the grave site. On the back of the stone, read "EGYPTAIR FLIGHT 990" and on the front, etched in gold, read in sections and different languages,

IN LOVING MEMORY OF THE 217 FAMILY MEMBERS AND FRIENDS LOST ON EGYPTAIR FLIGHT 990 CA 60 MILES SOUTH OF NANTUCKET ISLAND OCTOBER 31, 1999.

MAY GOD'S ETERNAL LIGHT SHINE UPON THEM

AND EVER HAS IT BEEN THAT LOVE KNOWS NOT ITS OWN DEPTH UNTIL THE HOUR OF SEPARATION
                      "THE PROPHET" KHALIL GIBRAN

It goes on to read in two other languages.

Front of the headstone in local cemetary of Newport, Rhode Island

Back of the headstone in local cemetary of Newport, Rhode Island

After the ceremony, the casket was closed and was lowered into the ground.

Soon after this time, a local state legislator from Rhode Island did all the families a big favor and was able to pass a law or take legal steps that declared all people aboard the flight legally dead. Otherwise, since no survivors were found, they would be declared missing, and we would have had to wait out the declared number of years for a person who has gone missing and was never found to be declared legally dead. The act of the legislature allowed everyone to move forward to start to settle the estates of the passengers. This also allowed for death certificates to be issued, which are needed to close accounts and all the other tasks that people must deal with when a person dies.

In January of 2000, certain relatives reassembled in Denver to start breaking down my mother's home. We had waited to do it as the holidays came right up after the crash, and we had to get through that emotionally before we tackled breaking up my mother's home.

I remember the first day. It was an extremely emotional time for me. At that time, I still really loved my mom. Only through therapy in dealing with my adopted mother's death did I go back over the years and re-examine my childhood up until the day she was killed. It was then that I realized she was a poor parent and made huge mistakes in raising me, and that's why I'm not sure I love my mom anymore. You could say I have a love-hate relationship with her.

The first room that we tackled was the guest room. In that room was a desk with many drawers. All the travel brochures and such were kept in the drawers from our many European and UK trips. It immediately stirred up fond memories of those trips, and I ran out of the room to my old bedroom, where I lost it. I started crying sort of heavily but tried to stay quiet as I did not want my relatives to know that I was suddenly shaken. After a few minutes, I gathered myself together as best I could and re-entered the room to help out again. I wasn't fooling anyone. They knew.

Breaking up Mom's house was extremely emotionally draining, and I never want to go through that experience again. Once was more than enough.

About a year after the plane crash, EgyptAir settled with all the families. My aunt Mary, when my mom died, was very greedy. She felt cheated that my mom did not leave her anything financially in the will. My mother logically didn't have to. It doesn't work that way. If a parent dies, in the normal scheme of things, they leave their assets and things to their kids. Aunt Mary disagreed with that school of thought.

So, before it was announced that EgyptAir was going to settle, Aunt Mary started to see dollar signs in her eyes. She wanted to sue EgyptAir and cash in big time. She found out that the famous lawyer, Jerry Spence, had a branch office in Denver. I'm not the suing type, yet she wanted me to go with her to meet with one of the attorneys in Mr. Spence's office. I don't remember the full details of the meeting, but the lawyer we met with did not seem enthusiastic. Maybe he knew something we didn't that it may be hard to prove beyond a shadow of a reasonable doubt that we would have an airtight case. It wasn't long after that I was contacted by letter from a law firm in New York City, and their firm was handling a class action lawsuit representing many of the families. So, the Jerry Spence endeavor was dropped.

It was obvious I was going to receive a payout from EgyptAir, even though I personally was not looking for one. Once I knew of the payout amount, Aunt Mary started applying extreme pressure on me that she wanted a chunk of that payout. Her excuse was that she was my mom's sister; therefore, she felt entitled and was due some money, especially since my mother did not leave a thing to her.

My birthday came along in April, and my mom and I had a tradition that we would take each other out for dinner on each other's birthday. Since my mother was no longer with us, and it was my first birthday since the crash, Aunt Mary stepped up and took over the tradition for my mom. While we were eating dinner, she brought up the fact that she again wanted some of the settlement money. She looked at me intensely, gritted her teeth as she spoke through them, with a clenched jaw, uttering the words "Bill, don't you get greedy!" in a nasty tone. My first thought was, *F**K YOU!* Obviously, I did not say that, but I was strongly thinking it. I wanted to say right back to her face, "Mary, DON'T *YOU* GET GREEDY!" Needless to say, she ruined my birthday dinner.

When the payment came in, I gave half of it to my sister. I personally did not want to give Aunt Mary a dime of the settlement, but I was still not thinking clearly as I wasn't myself and still not over the grief of Mom's death. It took about a full two years till I was back to my full normal self again, where I could think soundly about family matters involving issues that were still happening as a result of my mom's passing.

Since Mary was putting so much pressure on me for a chunk of the settlement, and I still wasn't of sound mind yet, I foolishly offered her a figure, and she accepted it. So now, I created another dilemma for myself. Since I gave Aunt Mary a portion of the settlement, I now had to give the same amount to my mom's other sister, or I might have been accused of playing favorites. So, I ended up giving my mom's other sister the equivalent amount, and as a result, I didn't end up with much of the settlement thanks to *GREEDY* Mary. If I had a chance to do it over again, I would have told Mary to go pound sand; I'm not giving her a cent. She was not part of our immediate family.

My birthday dinner with (from left to right) Aunt Mary, my adopted mom, and me.

Chapter 19

Trying to Move Forward By Climbing Emotional Mountains

Getting through the first set of holidays after my mom's passing was difficult. Holidays would never be the same going forward. Because of the emotional loss of Mom, my OCD became intense. It was as if I fell off a metaphoric cliff and was out of control washing my hands, and people were noticing. As of this writing, it's been twenty-four years since the crash of EgyptAir. I remember how badly the OCD was affecting me. It was paralyzing my life. However, having to deal with a life-changing event caused much anxiety and made my OCD worse. I had to ask people around me when I had touched an item that I felt was contaminated and if I needed to wash my hands.

If you don't have OCD, it's hard for you to relate. If someone with OCD is reading this, they understand perfectly what I'm talking about. To refresh your memory from my chapter on OCD, it is also known as the "Doubting Disease." Because our OCD brains are formed differently, we seek reassurance because we have difficulty differentiating between what reality *actually* is and what our minds tell us reality is. If I don't get clarification from someone, the need to wash my hands grows ever greater. That's why I have an overwhelming need to wash my hands to get the contamination off and feel clean again.

Relatives could all see how tormented I was and how I could barely function. They wanted to help me. I let them know of the OCD Institute near Boston, Massachusetts, and how they had a treatment center there where you could attend a program. Supposedly, they work with you to try to help make your life easier so you can learn to function with OCD.

As I was researching how to attend the OCD Institute, without my knowing it, my dear cousin Kim took her own initiative and found an OCD therapist who I ultimately found to be outstanding. Carrie Campen, my therapist, gave me my life back to the point where I can almost live like an OCD-free person.

Carrie had the answers to help me better myself to the point that OCD was not as bad as it had been. She brought me back from the edge to lead a somewhat normal life. Carrie is an expert in her field. She is the only person I've met who doesn't have OCD but completely understands the OCD mind and how it adversely affects people.

Since I had difficulty with everyday life due to the burden OCD had created, Carrie started making home appointments with me. She helped me in cognitive therapy in the forms of cleaning, touching things I felt were contaminated, and many other OCD obstacles that impeded my life. In addition, Carrie has been an excellent listener to my other issues outside of OCD that were roadblocks for me to enjoy life, and she provides great positive feedback that has increased my self-confidence. Before meeting Carrie, my life was so limited. I could not travel. I could go into detail, some I've already mentioned, but the nitty-gritty details are too personal to get into. Only people who know me extremely well know the difficulties that I face with OCD. While traveling, only on a few occasions have I had to call her from the road when I got embroiled in a real OCD disaster and started to freak out. I am not weak; I can reason well when it doesn't involve OCD issues. As the reader, I direct you to the Jack Nicholson film As Goods as It Gets, where he plays a character, whose OCD is debilitating. You could get at least an inkling of what I must deal with 24/7/365.

When Carrie started working with me, I was severely depressed for many reasons. I wasn't enjoying life, which probably goes all the way back to when my parents got divorced in the early 1970s. I was ready to die at any time. I didn't want to live anymore, having suffered the crap I've had to deal with in my life. I had been messed up for years over the rejection of Gertrude (and still am in some ways) and not able to find my purpose in life; I failed at many jobs because they were not the right fit for me, and suffered from *extreme loneliness*. I had a poor self-image based on my life's experiences of being unpopular and oftentimes always being the butt of jokes from the workplace to different groups of friends. I failed at romantic relationships and hated living in a cold climate that had snow. Because of how bad my OCD was, I was *unable* to move away. I felt trapped in Colorado, like I was stuck there forever while OCD kept me hostage. This and other issues I was dealing with led me to become irritable and frustrated of living where I didn't want to be.

After Mom's death and trying to cope with Gertrude's rejection, I turned into a very heavy drinker. At that time, I drank a twelve-pack of beer every night for five years. My tolerance was so high that I didn't even begin to catch a buzz till the seventh beer.

Due to my extreme depression, I tried to commit suicide three different times as an adult. I was trying to figure out my life and my purpose, wishing I had been aborted and resenting my birth parents for conceiving me because of everything I'd had to endure all my life with few positives. Remember, the first time I attempted suicide, I was in junior high after a huge argument with my mom.

I was living in my townhouse in Denver, and there were times when I felt so depressed that I could no longer go on. I had had it with life. I was of the mindset for years that I was ready to die. I was just not enjoying myself on this earth. I often felt that if I had a red button next to me, I could push it to end my life immediately. I would have pushed that button on so many occasions. I felt I had nothing to live for, no purpose or direction, just wasting away as each day went by. When I flew, I'd pray the plane would crash, and my life could just be over. Now, I did have compassion for my fellow passengers, and I did not want them to be hurt or die. I just wanted *my* life to end.

During these different episodes that occurred, I was feeling very distraught and absolutely helpless. I did not (and still do not) have deep enough friendships that I could call for support. Once, after a night of heavy drinking, I took a slew of sleeping pills, hoping never to wake up. Nothing happened. I woke up the next morning with no ill effects. The next time I was lying in bed in the middle of the night feeling completely helpless with no future. I got out of bed, put on my robe, went out to the garage, got in my car, and started it up. I rolled the windows down, and reclined the seat, and attempted to fall asleep, hoping the exhaust building up in the garage would kill me, and it would be a peaceful death. After about five minutes, I chickened out, went back into the house, and returned to bed.

Then, the next time I felt pushed to the edge of emotional peril, I was so distraught, again, in the middle of the night, that I went online to see what stores sold guns. I was going to buy a gun, shoot myself in the temple, and have it end quickly. I was trying to find painless ways to die. I researched the internet and thought sleeping pills would be the easiest. Turns out it's not. I learned that if you take a lot to make a viable attempt to end your life, it is always possible that you may miss the mark and experience pain as your body reacts to the high dosage of sleeping pills. Then you stand a good chance of vomiting, and if you *are not* successful and *live*, you may end up as an invalid with severe brain damage. It turns out after my internet search, I don't think there is any way to commit suicide pain-free. Even drowning is a very painful way to die.

I was getting quite serious about ending my life because I just didn't feel I fit in anywhere. I never really felt accepted by my classmates or in the jobs I held. For ninety percent of my life, I'd felt lost. Ironically, the only thing my adopted Dad and I had in common was that he told me he never fit in anywhere, either.

For many years, I held a strong resentment against my birth parents for having me. I felt they didn't think things through when it came to what my life would be like. I felt they thought, *Oh, wouldn't it be so nice and cute if we had another little child to have around.* And they probably would have assumed I'd have a happy life and be successful, and everything would work out. Then I've pondered if I was an accident and that's why I'm here. If they were alive today, I would ask them that.

I have gone up and down with depression most of my life. I asked a therapist once if I was bipolar, and she said no. I remember when I was fifteen, sitting at my desk in my room, doing homework, and I stared out the window. I remember declaring myself officially depressed. That depression lasted till I was fifty-nine. I have written many poems and lyrics over the years about the deep emotional pain I've dealt with.

While in therapy with Carrie, soon after my mom died, I went back over my childhood up to the day Mom died in the airliner and reviewed how she treated me. Mom had done a lot of good things for me, but the bad things and her philosophy of raising my sister and me outweighed the good. Toward the end of her life, when I was so depressed, she used to say, "I'm your number one fan." I didn't quite fully buy it. Anyway, I went into deep detail with my therapist about how I was raised and concluded that I no longer loved my mom. Through the course of writing this book, I have re-evaluated my feelings. I realize I have a love/hate relationship with her. But still, it leans more toward the hate side.

Up till the time I met Carrie, I had always tried to seek other people's approval because I never got any. Therefore, I have spent most of my life trying to please my mom by doing the things *she* wanted me to do *instead of what I wanted to do*. I really need to feel accepted.

I have never had much self-confidence over the course of my life. My father constantly lectured me about how I was never doing things right and made me feel I could never live up to his approval. I tried to get my mom's approval by doing what she wanted. Women have always rejected me. I was bullied at school and in the workplace and have had few friends. You can see how I got to the point of having severe depression. On top of that, OCD was thrown into the mix. This causes a lot of obstacles to deal with that most people have not experienced. I *so* wanted people's approval and tried to get it by doing what *I thought* they wanted me to do, and I couldn't be myself.

So, along came Carrie. By working with me, *she literally gave me my life back*. She got me back to the point where I could travel, build up my confidence, and completely understands how bad my OCD was; she knew how to make my life easier to cope with it, so that I could function again like the average person. On many levels, now I can do things a normal person can do without having to freak out about it. I must do them in a different way, and it takes me longer, but I can do them.

Carrie brought me out of my shell, allowing the real me to shine through. Do what *I* want to do instead of trying to get approval from others doing what they think I should do. She got me to have the appearance I want and not bow down to how society tells me how to look age appropriate. Since I was a kid, I have always wanted long hair, so I grew my hair out into a ponytail. I also grew a beard. I've received some pushback from people who wish I'd go back to the clean-cut look, but if I did, I would *not* be true to myself. I'd be caving to the approval of others. My attitude nowadays is that people *must* accept me as I am or not at all. I don't want to be boxed into that cookie-cutter mold. I have to be me. A large part of me does not want to conform to expectations. It's the rebel in me being exposed.

I believe that for every negative that happens, you can always find a positive if you look hard enough. In the case of my mom's airline crash, the positive of that negative was that I found Carrie (via my cousin Kim). Carrie has brought me to a good place through much hard work, doing my best to get me to the point where I can enjoy life again and do the things I couldn't do before.

Carrie even got me to the point where I could escape Colorado and move to a coastal community where I am now thriving, and my heart and soul have always really belonged. Surfs Up.

Chapter 20

Poetic Justice

My relationship with my dad remained strained after my mom perished in the airline crash. It was always a hollow relationship. We never shared any common interests to bond over. Dad never knew who I really was. We never connected as father and son.

I remember after Dad's third divorce; I visited him in Florida. That's when I first learned he had a hidden talent where he could draw portraits of people. He was quite an accomplished artist. He even drew me from a photo he had. I have to say he drew a wonderfully detailed portrait of me. Unfortunately, I cannot hang it as it would remind me of him every time I looked at it, and that would lead to feelings of anger. I was very impressed by his talent. I can't draw that well. Why he never mentioned in all that time he had that gift, I will never know. I like to draw, too, but my drawings are of cars I've designed, using rulers and drafting tools to create the lines I'm after. I don't think he knew I drew. He briefly explained the tricks to drawing portraits. Looking back, I wish I could have discussed drawing with him in more detail.

The few nice things Dad did for me over my lifetime were very few. I could count them on my fingers and still have some left over. There were three that really stood out that I really enjoyed. The first one was when I was a junior in high school. On spring break, he and a co-worker gave me a private tour of the steel mill for the company he worked for in Kansas City. It was very educational. I really enjoyed that. At the time, I remember thinking *I want to be just like him. I want to go to work for this same company* because, at that time, I still had some love left in me for him.

Me and my adoptive dad at Cape Canaveral prior to the launch.

The second thing was that since my dad lived near Daytona, Florida, and I've always loved auto racing, I told him I would like to come down to see the Daytona 500 live. He couldn't get tickets, but he did the next best thing and got tickets for the race the day before, which had all the same drivers. He even went the extra mile and rented a video camera so I could film it. The movie *Days of Thunder* had just been out a few years. For those who haven't seen it, it is a teaching film about NASCAR and the skills needed to stay competitive on the track. Dad knew little about auto racing, so I tried to create a bonding moment. I brought a couple of documentary VHS tapes (pre-DVD age) about the making of *Days of Thunder* and another by NASCAR driver, Darrell Waltrip, where he explained what it felt like from a driver's perspective. Both are very educational. I thought this would give Dad a better understanding than watching cars drive around the track. He had zero interest in watching them. It totally blew the opportunity to bond.

The third great thing he did for me was when I finished my internship in Washington, D.C., in the early 1980s, I drove south to New Smyrna

Beach, Florida, to stay with him, which ended in me abruptly leaving after about ten days when he started lecturing me on some fault he thought I had. However, prior to our falling out, he got passes for the seventh launch of the Space Shuttle flight. It was a history-making flight as it was the inaugural flight of Sally Ride, the first American woman in space. I'm a huge fan of the space program, as well. The passes got us onto the grounds of Cape Canaveral. We watched the shuttle take off from about one mile away. That was one of the two greatest days of my life.

After my adoptive Mom was killed, we did not communicate much. Talking by phone was basically non-existent. Then, on December 16, 2004, after not hearing from him in a long time, out of the blue, I got this bizarre email from him that crushed me. It reads as follows — typed verbatim with misspellings and all.

Subject line: 'Goodby'

Over the last few months we havnt emailed each other very often and when we have it has only been to exchange pleasentries, I assume that you have either reached a point in your life that you feel self-suficficient (which is great) or you have fallen back into some past habits. At any rate it is time and important for you that I say goodby as your father and look to my own personal interest. I do love you but believe that parting is best at this time. If you should ever need me please call. Im sure that you will not understand this today but hopefully you will some day. with love..goodby..your dad

What the hell is this? I thought. I immediately fell to the floor and started crying my eyes out. *What was it that I did that was so wrong? My adoptive mother was killed, and now you are deserting me?* At this point, I had lost all four parents I was dealt. I also became angry and felt more isolated. *I had three parents who were killed, and now my adoptive dad is disowning me. Why?* I kept wondering. I had no idea what the hell he was talking about in the email. What past habits did I fall back into that he was referencing? Then he was contradictory in the email, saying if I ever needed him to call, yet he wants to cut off all communication with me? There he goes again, thinking about himself and not considering the feelings of the people he hurt. What kind of parent would cut off all communication with his kids and disown them? I made a decision right then and there I would boycott his funeral whenever he died. Up to this email, I had given my father a D, but after this email, I gave him an F minus. God, this hurt, and to this day, I have not understood why he did this, but he indicated he hoped I would someday. Well, I'm still trying to figure it out, and I'm still coming up empty. By the way, my sister got a similar email. I met with my therapist the following day. I explained to her the email I had received, and her impression of me that day was that I appeared to be shell-shocked and looked really sad.

Many years went by after receiving that email. Around 2016, I got on the internet to see if he had died. I was hoping so. That may sound odd to you, but I wanted to know if he was dead because if he were, I knew he could no longer hurt me anymore. My research uncovered that he was remarried. Remarried? This would be his fourth go-around at marriage. I was hoping, at least, that if he were still alive, he'd be in the old folks' home, dependent upon others.

I was informed by a source around this time that Dad was in the hospital near his last days, fighting cancer for the past five years. That's when I thought, *Poetic Justice!* That may sound cold to you, but I felt it was *KARMA* for all the crap he had put me through and deserved it as a major failure as a father. I did not have any sympathy for him, which goes to show the dislike I had for him. He *chose* to be a terrible father and *chose* not to get to know who I really was. That's on him.

I got the call on October 11, 2016; he had passed away. I got teary-eyed but I did not cry. I was a bit sad for about thirty minutes, then not so much. I was still a bit stunned. Even though no love was lost on my behalf, he was still my dad, and it's a strange feeling to know your parents are now dead. At first, when I absorbed the news, I now had none of my four parents alive anymore, and it gave me a weird feeling. For example, you can never get in trouble with them again; they no longer have any control over you or tell you how to live your life. It was simply weird for me. I could do anything I wanted and never hear any pushback from them. The downside is that they are no longer around with whom to seek advice. In my case, Dad was dead to me back in 2004, the day I received his screw-off email. The news I received on October 11, 2016, just made it official. I felt a big sigh of relief, and a burden was now lifted that I knew he could never hurt me again. When I became aware he was ill, I never had the desire in his last days to see him. I would have, though, under one condition: If he were willing to apologize for the evil way he treated me, I would have gladly gone. We could have made peace between us and ended things positively. However, I know my dad and know he would never apologize, even if he felt he knew he had wronged me. That was not who he was. In fact, I do not remember at any time, over the course of the time I knew him, that he apologized to me for anything. For the record, my dad did not leave anything to my sister or me in his will.

One of the first things I did after getting the news was to call my aunt in California, who was the only person I knew who was still alive and aware I did not have a good relationship with my dad other than my sister and knew that he had disowned me twelve years earlier. At *that moment,* I really needed someone to talk to who knew my situation. When I called my aunt, I said, "My dad just died."

I was expecting some support along the lines of "Oh, I'm sorry to hear that" or "Are you gonna be ok?" but instead, my aunt responded with, "Bill, why are you still letting this bother you?" *What?* I certainly did not expect that kind of non-sympathetic response from her. She knew I did not like my father as I had made my thoughts clear over the past years to her. But c'mon, it is my dad's death we are talking about. Whether he was a good guy or a bad guy, he was still my dad, and I did feel a wee bit of a loss in my heart. Well, my aunt was not of any help. Getting the news was a bit unsettling, and I was restless. So, I got in the car and took a long drive to process the news.

Six years after my dad's death, while authoring this book, I learned new information from a credible second-hand source about why my father had disowned my sister and me. According to my source, what was told to me seemed pretty logical. After knowing that alleged answer, now the pieces of the puzzle finally come together after eighteen years. My sister and I could finally get some closure. It filled a large hole in my relationship with my dad; at least we *now* know why.

A little backstory is needed to let you know what was going on at the time of our relationship. My dad, according to what he told me, had a difficult life growing up with his father, as well. As a result, my dad was drawn to drinking at the age of ten. From his parent's liquor cabinet, his first drink was a highball. He became an alcoholic as his life progressed. He finally entered Alcoholics Anonymous (AA) when I was a junior in high school.

After my adoptive mother's death, I was in a really depressed state, trying to heal from that and get over Gertrude's rejection. As a result, as mentioned in a previous chapter, I was drinking heavily during that extremely low period of my life. I drank a twelve-pack a night for five years straight. During the few times I was in contact with my dad, I discussed how much I was drinking. He must have assumed I was a lost-cause drunk who had no hope to stop drinking. If this is what he truly felt, he misinterpreted my situation. I say that because at some point after that he cut me out of his life. I practically all but quit drinking on my own. I don't remember the exact year it was, but it probably was around 2009. Currently, I rarely drink at home. When I do drink, it's when I'm on vacation, out with friends, or attending concerts. I no longer have that desire to drink that I once had when Dad assumed I was a lost-cause drunk. Back then, I was severely depressed, had no desire to live, and was escaping through alcohol. Now, I'm living a much happier life and don't need to use alcohol to escape.

The source informed me that years earlier when I had sporadic contact with Dad, he was very big into AA. I was told that Dad and his AA group sought psychotherapy as part of their 12-step program. According to my source, his therapist was very adamant about codependency and inner-family entrapment. From what I've been told, the way I understood it was Dad's therapist gave advice to distance himself from people, places, and things, which created anguish and worry. That sounds like bad advice if you ask me when it involves cutting off all communication with your own kids.

My source said that my dad felt that AA would have been a way for him to connect with me, but only if I also joined the program and became sober.

Dad apparently felt that AA would have been his gift to me. The source thought he had convinced me to go to some meetings. No, Dad, he *never* convinced me to go to *any* meetings. I remember Dad *suggesting* I attend some meetings. Apparently, Dad thought I had spoken to my sister about this and thought she talked me out of it. *I don't remember my sister saying anything of the sort to me.* Dad followed the therapist's advice. My source went on to tell me in order for Dad to stay sober himself, I had to join AA, and if I didn't, he could not maintain contact with me. I was informed Dad felt he was in a "no win" situation since he could not convince me to follow his lead into the AA lifestyle. It was for this reason he decided to sever ties with me to relieve himself of the disappointment and frustration of not being able to get me to join AA. He blamed my sister for having that influence over me, and that's the reason he cut my sister off, as well.

After receiving this new information and learning the reason why Dad cut us off, I discussed it with my sister and realized it was totally unfounded. Neither my sister nor I ever remember a conversation between us where we talked about me going to AA, nor does she remember saying anything of the sort of her trying to talk me out of it. As far as my sister and I are concerned, that conversation never took place. That was *just* like Dad jumping to conclusions and making his own assumptions without understanding all the facts. Due to Dad misinterpreting the facts of the situation, my sister and I were cut off from communication for the last twelve years of his life, all because my dad misinterpreted and came to his own conclusion and made the wrong decision based on his poor reasoning and just assumptions. See, if Dad really knew us, there would never have been this breakdown in communication, and we may have saved our relationship from Dad taking uncalled-for extreme actions.

Honestly, I quit drinking altogether because I had such a high tolerance that I couldn't catch a buzz anymore, and I really started disliking the taste of beer. And that's when I quit. It was probably around 2009. There was a chunk of years that can be singled out, including some years before my mom's death, when I went through the roughest period of my life. It was during those dark days that Dad disowned me. With Carrie's positive help, I turned my life around, and I'm in a whole new place mentally than when Dad ended the relationship. It is his loss.

Once I tried to share some of my poetry with him, I wrote from deep emotional pain. After reading it, he just handed it back to me without saying anything. That hurt. I pour my guts out in most of my poetry; I think it's deep. To not even give any feedback, whether it is positive or negative, made me feel I wasted my time showing him what I had put deep thought and time into writing. I hoped he might want to ask me questions about what I felt through my writing so he could understand me better. I *just* could *not* connect with that man! My dad was a one-of-a-kind, self-centered bastard, and the world evolved around him.

My dad was a very flawed man, perhaps because of his upbringing. I really long for what our relationship *could* have been. I know I have ragged on my father, deservedly so, but I still wish we could have been best buddies. I had worked so hard over the time I was in touch with him in different ways to connect, but as it played out, he was only interested in *his interests,* and since I really did not share any of those, any chance of us becoming close was futile. I'm so glad I am not like him. Our personalities are so different. He was a hard man to please and a really difficult man to get along with. To this day, I still have no regrets about boycotting his service, and I'd do it again if he died today. What a crappy father he was!

Chapter 21

Shaken to the Core

About a year after my adoptive father died, something else happened to me that shook me to my core. It was worse than losing my mother in the plane crash.

I have always been a cat lover. We also had two dogs while I was growing up. I like dogs, but much prefer cats. I don't believe in reincarnation, but if indeed we *are* reincarnated, then I'd like to come back as a cat to a nice family.

Because of my OCD, having a cat has been difficult when it comes to dealing with cleaning a cat box. One of the chores I had growing up was to clean the cat boxes every week. Now, I'm not talking about just sifting through the kitty litter. I had to empty out the two cat boxes we had into the trash can. Then Mom had me take the hose and stand out at the curb and hose both out. Well, when I did that water would splash out of the cat box and sometimes land on me. That's where *one* of my OCD issues comes into play. My OCD causes me to have *transfer contamination issues*. You see, when I hosed out the cat boxes, some remnants of cat waste would splash on me. Well then, it would make me feel contaminated and the need to change clothes. Otherwise, I felt like I was walking around with cat waste on my clothes.

In addition, OCD played a *second* factor when sifting out the cat box. My OCD mind would tell me that I placed both of my bare hands in the dirty cat litter and moved them around. After a few years of getting our second cat, Boots, it is about the time I developed OCD. Eventually, I could not do the cat box chores and had to explain to Mom that I felt so dirty cleaning them (unless I wore a hazmat suit, in which case, I'd be totally fine cleaning them, LOL). It was just too emotionally stressful for me. From that day forward, Mom took care of the cat boxes.

At the time of the plane crash, Mom had a cat. She was Siamese, approximately ten to thirteen years old and in perfect health. Her name was Opal. Mom gave her that name because of her beautiful eyes. I called her Opie. Due to my OCD issues with cat boxes, I could not take Opie. Within a few days, one of my mom's friends agreed to take her. I hated to see her go. I would have kept her if it wasn't for that pesky OCD!

A few years after meeting Carrie, I wanted to get a cat, but I couldn't deal with a cat box. With Carrie's help, she worked with me on my cat OCD issues. Thanks to electric cat boxes that took care of the cat box problem. The electric cat box would scoop up the waste automatically into a receptacle. Therefore, I only had to throw out the receptacle once a week. That I could deal with.

Now, the new cat box more or less solved the OCD issues of having a cat. At this point, I was on the verge, ready to get a new cat. Carrie had the idea of going to a rescue shelter to *just* look at cats and hold them. Well, I knew in my heart was not leaving without a cat. I was ready.

I picked out this one-year-old grey cat with some white on her face and belly. When I held her, she went limp in my arms. That solidified it for me. This is going to be my new cat. I named her Smokey. I was still experiencing what seemed like never-ending depression, and just having her around lifted my spirits. Smokey and I developed a very close bond. Years went by with no issues of contamination. However, when Smokey was young, the vet discovered she had an enlarged heart that had to be monitored over the years. In her old age, she was vomiting quite often. The vet wasn't sure what was causing it, so the vet called a roving cat heart specialist who would go from vet to vet. What happened next is that my life would be shattered a third time. When I took Smokey to the vet to be seen by the heart specialist, I had no idea this would be the last day I would ever see her.

The day of Smokey's appointment was January 17, 2017. It was a cold winter day, and it had just snowed the night before. The heart specialist was to come between 2-4 p.m., but the office said to bring Smokey in around 1:30 p.m. just in case the heart specialist arrived early. That's what I did. Smokey was only supposed to be there for basically two hours, so I did not go home. Instead, I spent the two hours doing errands and such. I finished early, about 3:30 p.m. When I returned to the parking lot and waited, I had yet to hear from the vet, so I figured the heart specialist hadn't come yet, and I'd patiently wait in the car and listen to the radio. It was warm enough that I did not have to run the engine to provide heat. Well, four o'clock rolled around, and I still had not heard from the vet. I called the vet's office from my car to check Smokey's status. The vet told me the heart specialist hadn't shown up yet. *What?* I thought. The vet called the heart specialist, and she had forgotten about my appointment. So, she rushed out. Finally, the vet's office called (I was still in my car listening to the radio), and Smokey was ready to be picked up.

It was now dark out at about 5 p.m., and I took my cat carrier and picked up Smokey. I got back to the car, and I had Smokey's interest in mind and let her out of her cat carrier so she could be free while we drove home. Smokey was acting wild, very erratic, as I had never seen her like this before. Like a monkey, she was jumping all over the car and the dashboard. She was obviously very distraught, having been cooped up in a cage for the last four hours. And that's the entire reason I thought she'd enjoy her freedom from the cat carrier on the drive home.

I went to start my car (which I bought new only one year earlier). The battery was completely dead! I thought, *that's not supposed to happen with a new car!* Being a new car, I did not feel I needed to have jumper cables with me. I went to buy some at the grocery store in the same parking lot. On the way out of the store, I asked politely if I could get a jump from a guy, and he flat-out refused. Then there was a nice guy who said yes. Mind you, where I was parked, it was very dark. No lampposts from the lot were close enough to shine a light on my car. I told the gentleman I had to open the car door and pull the lever for the hood. So, I knew when I opened the door, Smokey would try to jump out. Since I could not see well, I opened the door just a bit to pull the hood lever. At the same time, I tried to block the open area between the door and the car with my body. I couldn't see a thing in my car due to the darkness, and sure enough, I felt Smokey's little body slide past my legs. I immediately told the guy, "Hey, I have to get my cat." He responded in an angry tone, "You can find your cat later; let's jump your car now." I was torn.

Both jumping my car and looking for Smokey were immediate equal priorities. I had to make a choice. Since the guy was there jumping my car, I went with that option. Once the car started, I went to look for Smokey. It was now even colder outside. I was searching all over the whole parking lot calling her name. I was down on all fours, looking under cars to see if she was hiding. The knees of my jeans got soaking wet from the slush and the previous melting of the snow mounds the plow drivers had piled up in different spots around the parking lot. I had zero luck. Meanwhile, I had a near-empty gas tank. I thought the only thing I could do now was go home, make signs, and return and post them in the parking lot. Before I could leave the parking lot, I stopped for gas at a station located in the shopping center. I began filling up my car and realized I was getting a free tank of gas. Being the honest person I am, once full, I hung up the nozzle and went inside the gas station to see the cashier. I explained that I just got a free tank of gas, I wanted to pay for it, and indicated that someone before me at the pump must have left it on or something for me to get the free tank of gas. He started going through the receipts and found mine, which indicated that *I had paid* for the gas. *I did?* I thought. *I have no recollection of inserting my credit card into the pump.* It was then I realized what was happening. I was going into shock over my distress of losing Smokey. I had to rush home, approximately twelve miles round trip, and grab some copy paper and a marker and makeup about seven quick sloppy lost cat signs. I would make a better one the following day. I was in emergency mode. I loved Smokey as if she were my child. I was so protective of her that I considered her my daughter.

I made it back to the parking lot. By this time, most of the stores were closed, and the parking lot was becoming empty. I searched and searched. I even went behind the stores where the dumpsters were, and the delivery trucks came. Still no sign of Smokey. I gave up for the night at 9 p.m. after about four and a half hours of looking for her over and over, scouring the parking lot. When I left, it was getting *really cold*. It got down to 17 degrees that night, and I felt really guilty because here I was in a nice warm house, and Smokey was out there freezing.

The next day, I planned to get to the shopping center at 7 a.m. before people got to work and filled up the lot. Still no sign of Smokey. I went back to that parking lot eight separate times over a period of two weeks, combing it with a fine-tooth comb. I went both during the day and night. I took food and left it out. The vet told me to bring her cat box and put it outside because Smokey might be able to identify a familiar scent. The missing cat signs I put up all over the parking lot (which were all taken down by the businesses — their excuse was that they were not allowed to have signs like that on their windows). My signs were even taken down from the lamp posts in the parking lot. I searched a few nearby neighborhood streets day and night with a flashlight. I knocked on doors and checked nearby roads to see if she got run over. I put ads in several local papers for three months, including online social media sites, and I was checking shelters (and Smokey was chipped). I spent close to $1500 on all the sources searching for Smokey. I had a few leads, but they were never Smokey.

During the first week of losing her, I called a few friends and said I'm not taking any calls. It was like losing a family member again. I was not myself for three months. For the first three weeks, I put *everything* on hold, paying bills and whatnot. I was focused 100% on finding Smokey. She meant everything to me. She was my rock. She kept me going when I was depressed. She was my little buddy, and I *needed* her company. To this day, I feel guilty that I killed her in an indirect way. It's like a guy texting on his phone while driving and not noticing people in the crosswalk hitting and killing them. I must live with that guilt for the rest of my life. I'm still mad at myself for making that stupid mistake by letting her out of her cat carrier.

Fast forward to 2019. Now, I have moved to the East Coast. I bought a house with the emphasis that there would be a place for a cat box. There was. I determined a closet would work. Carrie worked with me, preparing me for when I would get a cat. I had been working on this dilemma for four years. I had almost come to the conclusion that because of my OCD, I would never be able to have a cat again.

BREAK THROUGH! I found a grey cat on a social media site that I couldn't live without. After two weeks, she was still available. She was a tiny kitten, and I realized I had better try to get her before someone else did. On December 1, 2023, I picked her up. I named her Smokey, as well. She is a keeper! She cuddles/sleeps with me, and we are an excellent fit. She is my sixth cat. If it were not for Carrie's OCD help, I could have never gotten a cat. *THANK YOU, Carrie!*

Now you are probably wondering how I am coping with the cat box issue. Well, I buy the flimsy cat boxes that are disposable, and I just throw out the whole box when warranted. It turns out that during those first weeks, I was sifting out the cat box and not having any contamination issues. Hopefully, it will stay this way. Extra shout-out to Carrie: Without your help, this would never have been possible.

My original Smokey who went missing

Chapter 22

Jack Pot City

"Changes in Latitudes, Changes in Attitudes"
— JIMMY BUFFETT

Colorado was never a good fit for me. I've found the landscape and the aesthetics unappealing to my eye. The only part of Colorado I care for is the Dillon/Vail area, which is only in the summer months after most of the snow has melted. The beautiful mountains and wildflowers make for wonderful photos of the landscape. I detest the Colorado winters. I have lived in a snowy climate basically all my life from when I was born till 2019. In all those years, not once could I ever get used to the snow and cold. The earliest I've seen snow in Denver is the first week of September, and the latest is the last week of May. That is not typical, but it happens. In my personal opinion, Colorado only has three warm months out of the year—June through August.

Many Coloradans will disagree with me, but I consider warm, comfortable weather to be 90 degrees and above. I really enjoy the hot weather, and I'm naturally a person who can get cold easily. Cold weather in the winter months makes me irritable. I don't handle cold weather well. I've never liked shoveling the snow, brushing it off my car, walking through slush, or having to drive by negotiating the snowy/icy roads. No, thank you. Some people love snow, but it's never been for me. I've never cared for a change of seasons. I prefer warm weather year-round. Where I now reside in South Carolina's Grande Strand, the winters aren't that cold, in my opinion. Long pants and sweatshirts are all I need to get through. For the most part, I've found I can wear short pants nine months out of the year. There are always a few days in the winter that are warm enough to wear my summer attire.

One winter, while in college, I got so fed up with the cold and wanting summer to return I channeled my frustration into the following poem.

Tragedy, Survival, and Triumph

Summer vs. Winter

Summertime is the greatest season of all
And snow refuses to fall.
The vegetation, such a deep rich green,
What an incredible scene!
When the temperature may hit 103
I feel like sailing the sea.
Wearing my sandals and shorts
As the top goes down
I sail through the wind in my sports car,
Worshiping every minute of this paradise.
And one quick thought of winter
I have absolutely no doubts at all
The heat is here to stay!

Winter, I loathe the most.
Colder than Hell could be hot.
For several months I sit and rot
Freezing in a barren cold desert.
I must sit and wait it out.
Waiting for that day
When summer comes back this way.
I bundle up, and I still freeze.
The snow melts, and the temperature remains at 34
And the climate screaming for more.
I wait in flustered anger
For the return of those scorching days.
That climate of California
Draws me closer every day!

-WILLIAM COWELL DUCKWORTH
Written between January 7 and February 14, 1983

I'm not sure where I lived the first nine months before my biological parents were killed, probably in California, as I was born in Long Beach. Then, once I was placed with relatives, I lived the next four years of my life in Minnesota. In 1964, my adopted dad was transferred to Denver with his job. There, I remained feeling trapped in a land-locked state until I escaped to Myrtle Beach, South Carolina, in April of 2019 at the age of sixty. Since I was a kid, I have always wanted to live near the beach. Surfing has always appealed to me much more than skiing. Yeah, I've tried skiing approximately seven times; I don't understand what all the fuss is about.

My absolute number one requirement was that wherever I was going to relocate, it would have to have palm trees. They have always been my favorite trees. Myrtle Beach was not my original destination. It was San Diego, California. I have been there many times and always loved it there. It felt comfortable; the place I needed to be. Living by the Pacific Ocean, with no change of seasons, San Diego averages seventy degrees year-round.

With Carrie's help, I could travel again, previously restrained and held down by my OCD difficulties. I flew out to San Diego to do serious research. I drove through the suburbs, heading as far north as Oceanside to as far inland as Lemon Grove. I was canvassing the area to see what area of town I preferred best. Once I got back to Denver, I started running the numbers and had been on a San Diego realtor's website, getting market updates for years. This allowed me to evaluate what I could afford in the real estate market. I had also investigated state income and property tax rates and realized that once I put it all together, I was priced out of the market. It was a no-go. Having my bubble burst, knowing I couldn't afford San Diego, I felt shot down and trapped once again in Colorado, assuming I would end up in the old folk's home and die in Denver. Ugg!

Someone had suggested Myrtle Beach to me. At the time, I was not keen on the idea of the East Coast as I was naive about my knowledge of hurricanes. I did like Florida, having been there many times and traveling the state, including Key West, except for the panhandle. In the early '90s, I toured part of the state as a potential relocation spot.

Having grown up in the West, I assumed a category 1 level storm would do maximum damage. Not so. After living here for a few years, you get educated about hurricanes.

I started my research online, looked at areas in Florida and Myrtle Beach, and realized the real estate market was more than affordable. It was even more affordable than real estate in the Denver area. So, this was something to consider. I mulled the idea around for a few years, and then when I got word that Dad died, that was a wake-up call to me. It made me think of my own mortality and how I may have only twenty years left on this earth before I meet my time of death. And I thought about how long I could go before I go into the *home* and depend on people to get by because I could no longer care for myself.

Suddenly, I went into overdrive mode, considering I better do this while I can, or it will never happen. Around 2017, I made my first trip to Myrtle Beach for a week. On the third day I was here, I felt a revelation. *I WANT TO LIVE!* I thought to myself. At that moment, it seemed my depression that I had been carrying for the last forty-eight years had evaporated like smoke dissipating into thin air. I knew in my gut while here at the beach that it felt like paradise. I felt peace in my soul, and this felt like home. Remember, from age fifteen up to now, I was extremely depressed with suicidal tendencies. I love the beach life.

I developed a plan once I returned to Denver. I went online to real estate sites and started to investigate what type of place I could afford. In San Diego, I found a condo (which was nothing more than an apartment you had to buy) downtown. It was a tad nicer than an average apartment but nothing super fancy. It was selling for $500,000 and was only a two-bedroom with no real storage space.

In Myrtle Beach, back in 2017/2018, you could buy an extremely nice two-story home with a backyard for that. *WOW!* I also investigated state income taxes and property taxes and found out that it would be affordable in some ways cheaper than Colorado. I worked out an approximately two-year moving plan. That may sound like a long time to make a decision, but not when you hear about what was involved because it was a big move from one landscape to another. I wanted to feel confident in my decision and not move here and have regrets that I made a wrong decision or the wrong town. Once April 2019 rolled around, I was finally able to work out the logistics for both Denver and Myrtle Beach, and now I was ready to travel by car to do my test drive move. I had previously rented an apartment on one of my investigative trips to Myrtle Beach.

However, I had to stick around an extra two weeks for a very important reason near and dear to my heart. The Substitutes, Denver's own The Who premiere tribute band, was doing a show on Saturday night, April 20, 2019, at a bar in Evergreen, Colorado that's well-known for hosting live music. This would be my parting swan song and the last time I'd ever see them play.

On Monday, April 22, 2019, I set out by automobile for Myrtle Beach or bust. It is 1,743.7 miles from Denver to Myrtle Beach. I made it in three twelve-hour days of driving. I was motivated to get here.

My goal once here was all business. I was not here to play tourist, but I was on a serious mission with a goal to canvas Myrtle Beach and the local towns that adjoin it to see if I liked it enough to purchase a home with the intent before my lease on the apartment was up in September of 2019. I contacted a realtor, who came highly recommended. The first thing I immediately did after a day or two of getting settled was explore the Grande Strand to see what area I would prefer buying in, as I didn't want my choice to be limited to Myrtle Beach. If I only considered Myrtle Beach and bought there and then discovered a nearby town I liked better, I may have buyer's remorse, and I certainly did not want that.

I started my expedition at the border where North Carolina and South Carolina meet. From there, I zig-zagged my way all the way south to Georgetown, a total of fifty-four miles. I even went as far inland as Conway, approximately a thirty-minute drive west. In each town, I drove around, seeing what they were like. I gathered useful information by talking with the locals. You can learn a lot that way about the different areas. The expedition took me two weeks to complete. After assessing my evaluation, I chose Myrtle Beach itself because it seemed to have the most happenings going on and the fun that can be had downtown on the main drag called Ocean Boulevard.

I liken Ocean Boulevard to the Las Vegas strip. Not quite as bustling as Vegas, but for Myrtle Beach, it brought this town alive. I refer to Ocean

Boulevard as *The Mini-Vegas Strip*. In the evenings, it is swamped with locals and tourists who frequent bars, restaurants, and touristy stores; from early evening to the late-night hours, there is a traffic jam with cars moving at bumper-to-bumper pace for the main enjoyment of dragging the gut, showing off their cars or motorcycles they drive.

I had bought a spec home, so it was move-in ready before I returned back to Denver. I returned home to Denver in late August with the goal of selling my place by November 2019. The process of getting my Denver townhome ready to sell and figuring out what items I would take and leave behind were daunting. I wanted out of Colorado ASAP and to return to paradise as I saw it. I wanted to cut ties with Colorado and start a new, upbeat, promising future in the great state of South Carolina.

Moving to Myrtle Beach made all the difference in my life. I've discovered newfound happiness and a new reason for living. I try to get to the beach daily. It's always built into my daily routine. There is so much to do in the Grande Strand, more than what Colorado offered me with my interests. It's almost impossible to get bored here. Myrtle Beach has humidity, and I love it! Call me odd man out, but I prefer the feeling of hotter summers than what Colorado offers. I feel so lucky to have relocated here and to live the next chapter of my life in newfound happiness, and that's why I have nick-named Myrtle Beach "Jack Pot City."

Chapter 23

The Dawning of a New and Happy Life

Moving to Myrtle Beach was the best decision I have ever made. It completely got me out of my depression, and I'm very happy and *relaxed* down here. I've said for many years, "My soul was born at the beach," and the beach *is* where I naturally was supposed to be. I was so miserable in Colorado. It was *not* where I was *ever* meant to be. I'm all about living the beach life and wish I could have grown up surfing.

Since moving to the Grande Strand, I have developed a new interest in reading books I never did before because reading is so difficult for me. Nevertheless, I'm really getting into it and usually have three to four books going at a time. I have also developed a new passion for book writing. I have time to work on my lyrics and poetry. The beach always gives me the inspiration to do some writing. If something comes to me, it may only be a line, ideas for a song, or other book ideas to pursue. I always take a book and writing tablet to the beach with me. I currently have two more books I'm in the process of completing, and I hope to get those published, as well.

When I go to the beach, I like to prop my beach chair so I'm close to the incoming waves that wash up on the sand. I love the roar of the sound of the sea and the waves crashing. That is such a relaxing sound for me. I enjoy, at times, letting my mind drift off. I can break free of any stress or personal problems that I may have to deal with. When I leave the beach, my mind feels recharged, fresh, and more relaxed than when I went to the beach. You could say that the beach is the mental drug that I need on a daily basis.

Carrie knows me better than anyone on the planet, far better than either of my parents or friends. I have shared everything with her-all my problems and all my fears and issues. When she first met me after Mom's crash, I was not able to function well as a normal person. I was extremely limited in what and how I could do things in life due to the inability/grasp/lockdown OCD had (has) on my life. When she met me, I was suffering from low self-esteem (which had started when I was a kid). I had spent many years (from the mid-1990s to perhaps 2016) lying in bed all day, feeling hopeless, and living a failed life that was all due to severe depression, and Gertrude was the main reason for my *mass* depression. Still, it also had started long before she ever entered my life. I used to mask how I felt to everyone so that it appeared I was doing fine. It was only a cover-up/acting job on my part. On the inside, I was emotionally hurting. As mentioned in Chapter 14, a line from one of my poems reads, "On the outside, I contain a contented shell, but on the inside, I'm depressed as hell."

When Carrie came into my life circa the year 2000, that's when my life changed for the better. I was still a heavy drinker at that time. I didn't care about life and wanted to die. I was existing and not living. With Carrie's help and very hard work, I got my life back on track. Carrie got me to the point where I can handle *most* OCD problems on my own without totally freaking out and going into a full panic attack. With Carries' help, I had success, but it did not happen overnight. It was a long, long, hard road that I've been on, and I am still traveling that road to overcome most of my demons, which have gone from a dirt road to a paved one. I'm still a work in progress. I've been through a lot in my lifetime. I've had some really great times and have been able to do many things most people won't get to do. I may be financially secure, but I had to *pay a high price* because three out of my four parents had to be killed for that to happen.

Without Carrie's assistance, I'd still be living in Denver and probably be just as depressed as I was before I met her. It took me ten years of Carrie's therapy to reach the point where I wasn't constantly missing Gertrude and felt like a complete wreck over that loss from my life.

Years ago, Carrie, having heard me tell my life story and all the problems I've dealt with along the way, felt I had a compelling story to tell. She encouraged me to write this memoir and share my story on two separate occasions. When I gave it serious thought at that time, I could not bring myself to write it. If I did, that would mean I would have to go back and revisit the very painful emotional memories that I did not want to revisit because it would stir up the anger from the past and bring it to the forefront. I just couldn't do it back then. But then I moved to Myrtle Beach, and having a fresh, positive outlook on life, I felt I was *now* ready to tell my story.

I began writing this book in May 2020. While resurrecting bad memories of my past, there were times I got caught up in the heat of these ill-fated memories and became angry. I had to stop and walk away from the writing process, sometimes for two weeks. I had to let the stress level subside before returning to writing. This book has been very therapeutic to write. It has helped me make peace with my past and deal with my past anger.

Now, as this book is nearing its end, I no longer have so much anger and hatred toward my dad. Do I like him now as a result of writing about him in a therapeutic manner? *NO, I STILL HAVE NO LOVE FOR HIM,* but the anger now seems to have subsided, and let me tell you why.

While writing the Poetic Justice chapter on my dad, I learned why he had shunned me. Discussing the matter with a gentleman who was an acquaintance of my dad, I shared with him what it was like growing up with my dad and the evil he had inflicted on me. I shared the new information I received from my source about why Dad had cut off contact with me. This gentleman agreed that I had every right to be furious at my dad, and he validated my feelings of anger.

In addition, while writing that chapter, my sister, the acquaintance of my dad, and I all discussed Dad. The new perspective I have on my dad is that it was never really about me. It was all about him and his flawed personality; he was trying to make sense of it all and deal with his flaws that he projected onto my sister and me. I am still not letting him off the hook; he does *not* get a pass, but now I can at least find some inner peace with that portion of my life.

I have tried to write this book as the driver and have you, the reader, sit shotgun in the passenger seat as we've driven through the history of my life story, taking a side road or two and then getting back on the literary highway to continue the story. This has been a labor of love writing this book, and special thanks to Sandi Huddleston-Edwards for believing in me and wanting to publish my story.

One of the last times I saw my dad, I indicated I had never found my purpose in life. He said, "You will." It took me sixty-three years, but now I think I have finally found my purpose. *I AM A WRITER!* I'm *REALLY HAPPY* now.

So, that's my story, and I'm sticking to it!

Epilogue: After-Thoughts and Reflections

Well, now you have read the story of my life, I hope you like it and found it interesting. I tried to find humor where I could. There are certain things I've left out, but I tried to hit on the hard points that shaped who I became as a person and profoundly impacted me. It's been a tough road emotionally. I have worked hard to better myself and learn something new every day. In addition, I try to do at least one good thing a day for someone else.

I have been fighting a bit of guilt while writing this book, portraying the negative side of my adoptive mom. She did not always show her evil side to me. But it was there most of the time. My adoptive mom was rigid and stubborn. I can be stubborn, too, on occasion. We disagreed on how things should be done, resulting in many shouting matches. Nevertheless, I had to live with her for many years, and it was not an easy roof to live under with such tight control ruling my life. Once I moved out, she still tried to control me. Mom did do some nice things for my sister and me, such as taking us on trips around Colorado and for me to different places in the country. She was also extremely helpful in assisting with tasks that made the OCD side of my life easier. That being said, I still stand behind what I wrote about her.

The biggest question about life that I have going all the way back to junior high is why I have never been successful with women? I mean, it seems that having reached the age of sixty-four, I would have had at least *one* serious long-term *legitimate* relationship, yet for some reason, it has always eluded me. I feel I've been gipped on the limited intimate experience with women. I've never been the type to be promiscuous. I have taken dating classes, used all kinds of advice from my parents and friends, and

Epilogue: After-Thoughts and Reflections

even asked women what it was about me that turned them off. The women never really gave me hardcore answers as I think they were being nice and let me down easily and never wanted to tell me the truth. I once asked a woman out, and she laughed at me and said, "You're joking, right?" Up until my mid-fifties, I was asking women out. I have suffered so much rejection over my life from women that I won't even tend to approach women any more. I got turned down ninety percent of the time. I've seen videos suggesting that if a woman twirls her hair or other specific gestures, she is sending out signals that she wants to be approached. I would never pick up on any of those types of signals. I don't own a woman's manual of signals they send when they want to be approached. There's no class to take. So, being a guy, I have no idea that means they want to be approached.

It has more or less come down to the fact that if I am interested in a woman, then they must show me obvious signs that are blatant that they're interested, like an obvious smile, or initiated conversation, or let me know they're interested. I cannot read women's minds. As I've said previously, I haven't figured out the secret to attracting a woman. On my last few dates, which were years ago, I can't feel anything anymore romantically when getting ready or going out on a date as I've developed too much emotional scar tissue from rejection. I just feel numb when it comes to romance. It is so sad because I am a hopeless romantic, and I would want to spoil the woman of my dreams. On one occasion, I took a lady out on a first date to dinner. She informed me she had only gone out with me to get a *free* dinner. Obviously, at that moment, it was crystal clear she was not interested in me, and I got used.

The analogy I make is to imagine a wooden deck made from planks. Between the planks are small gaps. Now, imagine you have a handful of pebbles and throw them across the deck. Not all will land on the planks. Some, a very few, will fall between the cracks. The pebbles that remain on the planks represent couples, and the pebbles that fell through the cracks represent people like me who have never had the opportunity to have a legitimate relationship with a woman or success that leads to marriage. I'm the pebble who fell through the cracks through no fault of my own. It's just unfortunate bad luck. "I am an innocent man," sang Billy Joel, on "Innocent Man."

Epilogue: After-Thoughts and Reflections

It's impossible to say how my life would have turned out had my biological parents never been in that horrible automobile accident. However, I'm willing to put money down that I bet they would have been loving parents who would have known how to parent and not be like the two narcissistic parents who adopted my sister and me. My adoptive parents never encouraged us to be ourselves or were positive influences. They tried to mold us into them. I believe that had a deep-down psychological effect on me. Along with other bad experiences, I did my best to navigate my way through this life. One of the negative side effects left over from childhood still causes me to seek approval and want to be liked by others (I didn't always get positive encouragement from my adoptive parents), which outwardly projects a lack of self-confidence seen by others. My confidence is much stronger today, but I still need to hear that approval and be accepted.

My life has had its ups and downs and some really great moments. Surprisingly, I have been most fortunate to experience more than the average person. I love to travel, and my experiences have taken me to Europe, the U.K., Canada, Mexico, and Morocco, where my sister now lives. I still have a bucket list I'm working through.

The two most important things I have learned over my life are that I don't think I was meant to get married or be in a relationship, or it would have happened by now. The other is that I don't fit into the corporate world pushing paper. I was destined for creativity; i.e., the arts or music industry. Sometimes, I yearn for a second shot at life starting when I graduated high school. Having lived my life knowing what I know now, I would try taking a different route, perhaps the road less traveled. That's the school of life. Live and learn. I seem to have won in the end, though; I'm living my happiest days now than at any other time in my life. I'm where I want to be and can't imagine living anywhere else.

My biggest wish would be to have OCD vanish from my life completely, which would make my day-to-day life much more worry-free, and I could live like almost everyone else.

My two biggest regrets are as much as Gertrude hurt me, I still wish the relationship would have worked out. Second, I have never experienced true intimacy with a woman in a legitimate long-term relationship.

Epilogue: After-Thoughts and Reflections

My biggest fear is that I will die around the age of seventy, if not sooner. I've never felt I'd live a long life, going all the way back to my twenties. In January of 2022, I was diagnosed with an extremely rare tumor in my abdomen. It had to be removed. Luckily, it turned out to be benign; however, I still have to be checked twice a year for five years to ensure it has not grown back. My gut tells me I won't make it to old age like my adoptive dad, who died at eighty-seven, and my grandpa Ducky, who died at eighty-nine.

All that being said, I'm really happy, and my depression has vanished, and yes, the grass *is* greener on this side of the fence. God, I just love living the beach lifestyle! Flip-flops, short pants, and t-shirts.

"Catch a wave, and you're sitting on top of the world."
— The Beach Boys

And I'm riding that wave.

Resources

"2 Minute Neuroscience: Obsessive-Compulsive Disorder (OCD)." *YouTube*. 18 March 2022.

"3 Die In Auto Wreck." *The Washington Post,* 13 January 1960.

"3 Killed, 2 Orphaned By Crash." *The Miami News,* 11 January 1960, p.4.

"50 Famous And Successful People With OCD." *The Journal of Advanced Practice Nursing.* 15 February 2016.

"Aircraft Accident Brief." National Transportation Safety Board. 31 October 1999. pp. 3-5, 47, 67.

"Appointed To Annapolis."

"Arlington Burial Set For Cowell and Wife." *The Washington Post,* 13 January 1960, p. B2.

"Brewer's Son Killed In Crash: Young Cowell's Wife Also Auto Victim."

"Champion." *Sun-Telegraph Sports.* 1 July 1945, p2.

Cope, Myron. "Jet Pilot Bob Cowell Rejects Olympic Trip, Goes Off to War." *Pittsburgh Post-Gazette,* 5 July 1952, p. 9.

Resources

"Cowell Breaks World Swim Record."

Cowell, R.E. "Essay: My Year In College." 6 October 1943. p. 15.

"Cowell Wins National AAU Swim Title."

Drum, Bob. "Bob Cowell Sets Swim Record at North Park: Navy Star Nips Mark in Backstroke." *The Pittsburgh Press,* 21 July 1946, p. 23.

"Flier's Swimming Skill Saves Life in Sea Crash." *Pittsburgh Sun-Telegraph,* 3 March 1952, p. 2.

Hamilton, T. J. *U.S.S. Arnold J. Isbell (DD869).* Letter. 1947.

"Head-On Crash Kills 3 At Athens." *The Atlanta Constitution,* 12 January 1960, p.5.

"How Does OCD Affect the Brain? What Part of the Brain Does OCD Affect?" *Pratap's Neuro & Child Psychiatry Center.*

"How OCD Affects The Brain." *Change Your Mind Change Your Life.*

Jaral, Lokesh. "What is OCD? What Triggers OCD The Most?" *Deasilex.* 16 March 2022. www.deasilex.com. Accessed 29 January 2024.

"Joint Rites Slated For Cowells; Killed In Georgia Crash."

Langewiesche, William. "The Crash of EgyptAir 990." *The Atlantic Monthly,* November 2001, pp. 41, 46, 48-49.

"Lcdr., Mrs. Cowell killed in accident."

Miller, Jimmy. "Annapolis Captain In Two Races."

Moskin, J. Robert. "Are young Americans AFRAID TO FLY?" *Look Magazine.* 9 September 1952.

National Institute of Mental Health. "Obsessive-Compulsive Disorder (OCD)." www.nimh.nih.gov. Accessed 29 February 2024. pp. 1-4.

"Navy Couple Is Killed as Cars Collide."

"Navy Couple Killed in Head-on Crash." p. 19.

"Navy Man, Wife Killed in Crash." *The Evening Star,* 13 January 1960.

"Navy Men Meet." *Sun-Telegraph,* 2 July 1949.

"Navy Officer and Wife Lose Lives in Crash."

"Navy Officer, Wife Killed." *The Pittsburgh Post-Gazette,* vol. 33, no. 141, 13 January 1960, p. 4; p. 19.

"OCD Newsletter." *OCD Foundation and MEND Association,* December 1996, vol. 10. no. 6.

"OCD and Genetics: The Hereditary Habit-Impulse." *Impulse Therapy.* 2010. www.inpulsetherapy.com. Accessed 17 March 2022.

"Olympic Star, Now in Navy, Cheats Death." *The Pittsburgh Post-Gazette,* 4 March 1952.

"S.E. Cowell's Navy Son And Wife Die in Crash: Two Grandchildren of President of Brewery Hurt in Georgia Tragedy." *The Pittsburgh Post-Gazette,* vol. 33, no. 141, 13 January 1960, pp. 4 & 19.

"Services Arranged For Navy Couple Killed In Crash."

"Shake Down and Operation Frostbite."

"Squadron's History."

The Who. "Your Senses Will Never Be The Same." *Tommy Movie Poster*, 26 March 1975.

"Winners in Swim Meet Exchange Congratulations." *The New York Times*, 31 March 1946, section 5.

Zingheim, Karl. "Odds and Ends in the Freezer: The Bearcat, Helicopter and Fireball." *Operation Frostbite*. www.midwaycurrents.org. Accessed 4 January 2022.

"Zoloft Receives FDA Approval for Treatment of Obsessive-Compulsive Disorder." *OCD Newsletter*. December 1996, vol. 10, no. 6.

About the Author

WILLIAM COWELL DUCKWORTH was born into a military family in Long Beach, California, in 1959. Not long after his birth, his life suddenly and drastically changed. On the morning of January 11, 1960, he was traveling with his family, where his father was taking a new position at the Pentagon in Washington, D.C. Without warning, they were hit head-on by another driver who crossed over the center of the road. William and his sister were instantly orphaned. It was at this juncture that his life was changed forever. Relatives adopted the two siblings.

From that point forward, William has lived a different and harder life than the average person. He has faced many obstacles that created quite a challenge for him. He's been knocked down, but he has always gotten back up and forged ahead. There were dark days and times when suicide seemed to be the only answer to end his emotional pain. However, despite all this, he forged ahead and came out the other side, overcoming his depression and other issues, and now he is very happy and living the dream.

William grew up and spent most of his life in Colorado. He has since relocated to the East Coast. He now resides in Myrtle Beach, South Carolina, and is retired. He enjoys living a relaxing lifestyle and craves spending time at the beach, traveling, writing, and loving music. He is looking forward to publishing more books in the future.

www.ingramcontent.com/pod-product-compliance
Lightning Source LLC
Chambersburg PA
CBHW050242010526
44107CB00032B/1379/J